THE VOICE OF
FAITH

The Awakening Begins

HEATHER M. LARRIBAS

ISBN 978-1-0980-0852-9 (paperback)
ISBN 978-1-0980-0853-6 (digital)

Christian Faith Publishing, Inc.
832 Park Avenue
Meadville, PA 16335
www.christianfaithpublishing.com

Printed in the United States of America

Contents

ADAM'S HOMECOMING

WAKING UP ON A WARM SUMMER DAY in July 2017, with the sun gazing through the curtains hitting my face, I rolled over to feel Adam lying next to me. Not believing what I was seeing and feeling, I began asking, "Am I dreaming? Is that really him?" Wiping my sleepy eyes, stretching, and yawning, I began pinching myself to make sure I wasn't dreaming. "It is real. He is really here. He has returned." With a smile on my face and seeing that he was here next to me made me feel like all my prayers had been answered and all the nightmares had come to an end.

Finally, being able to breathe again, "Thank you, God, thank you, God, thank you, God, for returning Adam back to us." I kept praising God with so much joy filled within my heart.

Not trying to make a lot of noise, I slowly climbed out of bed and went into the kitchen, where I started making breakfast for us. It had been a long time since I was able to make any kinds of meals for him, that I was happy to do anything. Surprising him by making his favorite breakfast, French toast and bacon with a tall glass of pulp-free Minute Maid orange juice was waiting for him. Setting the table and looking out the sliding glass door, beautiful Pikes Peak mountains in bright blue skies and the sun gleaming were looking back at me. I couldn't help but feel that God was winking at me, letting me know that he was watching over us.

Walking back into our bedroom with anticipation in waking him up was a first beginning of a new journey that we had been given.

I believe a lot of couples take for granted the precious moments that God gives us. We forget to see that each moment with our spouse, our boyfriend, or significant other is truly a "gift" from God. God has knitted each one of us in his love and has asked us to love one another with all our heart and to serve him in his name to bring glory to him.

"Adam, wake up. I made your favorite breakfast for you."

"Okay, I will be there in a few minutes," was his response.

A few minutes later, he came out into the kitchen wearing his black shorts and a gray T-shirt. Just seeing him walking toward me and feeling the presence of him around me made me even more appreciative of what God did for me. As he sat down, he looked out the window and too he could see how beautiful the day was. I prayed over our meal as we began to eat. I started making small talk about things in general. It appeared he was enjoying his breakfast as he wasn't saying much back to me, but I could tell he was listening. With so many thoughts running through my head, wanting to ask him questions about us, I refrained myself and just sat back and enjoyed him being in the moment.

Sharing with him that I was interested in writing a book about how God saved me and saved our marriage, he looked at me with a look of surprise on his face inclining to me he really didn't believe that I was serious about writing.

"Why would you want to write about us? No one would read it."

Hearing that, my response was, "I want people to know that God is real and that he can heal any of us if we choose to follow him. I want to help others and I want and need to serve him."

My faith had grown so much, and with the vision that God had given me two years ago of returning Adam on a hot summer day in July came true, I wanted to share with the world that God does hear and answers our prayers. The burning desire to do what God had asked me to do was brewing stronger inside of me.

As I finished putting dishes away and cleaning up the kitchen, I heard little footprints coming up the stairs. Eastyn, who was two and half years old, and Brystyn, who was just one, were excited to see their grandpa and went running into the bedroom where they found him getting cleaned up for the day. I could hear them laughing as Adam was talking with them both.

While putting away the butter and syrup, a quick flash of the vision of him returning came back to my mind. "He did return on a hot summer day in July. That feels right. He appears to want to be here for good, but why doesn't it feel like that I am not sure if I want him back?" This scenario played over in my mind all day. Trying to ask God for some answers and asking him to show me anything or to talk to me, God was quiet making me feel very uncomfortable.

Ashley came upstairs awhile later, and she could see that I was thinking about something, "What is it, Mom?" she asked. "Aren't you happy Adam is home?"

"Yes, I am. I just want to be sure that he is here for good. You know what I went through and I want and need to trust that this is over once and for all. I can't go through this again. I pray that God has brought him back for good. It's just something doesn't feel right. Some things do but other things don't."

Ashley hugged me and said, "It will be all right, no matter what."

Still reveling in the fact that Adam was home and that he chose to come back. I let go of the vision and enjoyed a nice day and evening with my family.

Watching television in bed, laughing, and holding one another, I began to feel more secure in us. Being able to connect with my husband on an intimate level was something I had longed for and I had promised God if he brought him back, I would never turn him away. Falling asleep in his arms comforted me.

Waking up the next morning, Daxx had called to ask his dad to drive him up to Wyoming for work. Looking at me, Adam asked if I would like to ride along. With no hesitation, I said, "Of course." Getting ready and heading to pick up Daxx, Adam suggested we all go to eat at a deli restaurant before the long drive that was ahead of us.

Before we left, Adam was cleaning out his truck when he brought in jewelry he had bought for Loren. "What do you want me to do with this?" I asked as he handed it to me.

"I don't care. Do what you want with it," he replied.

Looking at the ring and the two necklaces made my stomach turn. Seeing the ring especially confirmed to me the ring I had seen floating around the room in February of that year had come true. Adam did indeed bought her a ring. It wasn't an engagement ring but a blue sapphire ring with diamonds on it. The intention was there of some sort of commitment to her.

As we all sat down to eat, both Adam and Daxx were scrolling through their phones. I could see that Adam was on Snapchat and not expecting to see Loren's name pop up surprised me. So, with Adam not knowing, I went onto his Facebook page, and there she was, still a friend of his.

"Why is she still his friend on Facebook and Snapchat?" I asked myself. As I leaned over to him while he was scrolling on his phone, he seemed irritated and asked me why I was snooping. There's a red flag, I thought. Not saying anything else, we finished lunch.

While we were driving, I kept talking to God in my head, asking him what was all this about. All I kept hearing from God was, "I am still working on him. He's not coming back the same. He loves only you. He's so glad you stayed." Hearing comforting words from God made me calm but still yet confused.

After dropping Daxx off, we started heading back home. I felt that maybe I could talk to Adam about what I saw and express how I was feeling. Noticing I still felt scared to talk to him, I pushed through and asked, "Why are you still friends with Loren on Facebook? Why is she still on your Snapchat?"

He said, "It's no big deal. I will remove it when I am ready. I am here, aren't I?"

"Yes, you are, but why are you here? What made you come back this time?"

"I felt the need to come back," he responded.

"That was the Holy Spirit telling you to come home. See, God is communicating with you," I tried to explain. Adam just looked at me like he could care less on what I was trying to say, and I knew then not to push any further with this discussion.

"When can we go see your grandma? You promised her a ride in your corvette." I was trying to change the subject to something lighter.

"Let's go next month, on my next days off," Adam suggested.

"Okay, I will call Kitty [that is what everyone calls my mother-in-law] and make the arrangements." Immediately the vision of us driving to California in his corvette with my new purse flashed in front of me. I thought, "I know I am not crazy. God showed this to me months ago." Excited to see that yet another vision was coming true made me keep my eyes on Jesus even more.

Driving through a city, Adam noticed a church with three crosses and pointed over to them for me to look at. Seeing the lights on the crosses piercing through the night sky warmed my heart. It was like God was getting Adam's attention by showing him the three crosses that represents the trinity: Father, Son, and Holy Spirit. After returning from our long trip, we were exhausted and went right to sleep.

It was now July 19, 2017. God was so specific to me when he had me write, "Your heart is heavy tonight, but I am here with you. Please keep the faith." As I wrote, what I was hearing made me feel like more things were yet to come. I couldn't understand why each day I would keep hearing the same things when looking at Adam and seeing him here in my presence made no sense. "Why do I keep hearing this? He's next to me. I don't understand God." I would always question, which made me feel uneasy about us.

The days were drawing near, and it was time for Adam to return to work. Not wanting to let him go but knowing he needed to, worry started settling back in. "No, Heather, I am not going to let Satan back in and make me feel this way. God has this. I must trust him and know that he is doing all that he needs to do."

Staying focused on God and reading daily devotions helped me to ease my mind while Adam was away.

One day, I received a text from Adam out of the blue with a phone number and a picture of a publishing place. "Thank you, but I would like it to be a Christian Publisher." I texted back. "It is," he said in a text back to me. Shocked but happy to see that he had listened to me and came across this publisher, I knew it was a sign that God needed him to be a part of this book. This brought me back to one of my journal entries I had written a couple years back that God had told me that I would be writing books and that Adam would be a part of it. He added, "Adam PA?" I still questioned what it meant but knew in time God would reveal when I was supposed to know.

Not having yet started writing my book, but with each passing day, the Holy Spirit was pushing me toward writing. I would wake up in the middle of the night asking God, "How do I write this? I never wrote a book. Is this what you really want me to do?"

The next day was July 31, 2017, and as I did each morning, I began writing in my journal a new entry. God started telling me that my book would be published within six months, a woman was going to be my publisher, and that I would help many people with their faith and marriages. He then had me look down at my phone and it said 10:02 a.m. "That's strange. That is my anniversary date, October second." He began showing me what the cover would look like and he gave me the title "The Voice of Faith." "Wow! That's powerful."

I started playing in my mind on how I would begin writing my book. I jotted down ideas and words to help get the juices flowing. Each day, more ideas would come to me and I became more comfortable with the idea of writing. I knew deep down that our story was meant to be heard.

In talking with my friend Felicia, I shared with her all that had happened after Adam returned and she encouraged me to continue the path of rebuilding Adam and me. She herself was going through her own struggles that I also encouraged her to continue walking the path that God had put her on. Talking to each other each day and sharing scriptures helped keep us in good spirits and to continue to walk in the faith.

Meanwhile in the earlier months, Shawna and I talked about her getting herself baptized and encouraged her to do so. She had started reading the Bible and reading devotions to change outcomes in her life. She had been thinking about it for some time and knowing it was important to our mother, she decided she was ready to make the change for herself.

"Well, I did it," Shawna called one morning to share the good news.

"You did what?" I asked.

"I am getting baptized on August twenty-seventh."

"Good for you. I am so proud of you, sis. You will feel better and your life will never be the same."

"I'm scared," she expressed.

"I understand but just know that Jesus is with you and he is so excited for you, but I must tell you, watch out because Satan will test you even more once you give your life over to him. He doesn't want you to be saved. You will go through tests and God will continue testing your faith. Stay strong and know that I am here for you." I didn't want to scare her, but I remember when I had given myself over to Jesus, Satan would try to get me to read more tarot cards and try to get me to follow others. He would give me fearful feelings that would get into my head a lot of times to try and discourage me.

Baptism

It was now August of 2017, and Adam and I were packed and ready to head to California in his corvette. The twenty-two-hour drive was ahead of us, and I was excited to have all this time with Adam to myself in the car. Taking my computer to read to Adam my book along the way helped to break up the trip.

In reading the first part of my book, I had written about my childhood and sexual abuse with my step-father and the other relationships that were not good for me. I wanted to share with everyone not to be ashamed and that we all have stories that need to be shared to help others. There are times that we all have felt alone, scared, and were victims and traumatized in our lives.

While writing out all my feelings and letting go of the pain, somehow made me let go of what I had been holding on to that I hadn't realized all those years ago. I was able to really forgive all that I endured as a child and the people in my life who I thought didn't care. I was beginning to heal the little girl inside of me through Jesus. Jesus was giving me the strength to face all my fears and to allow him to heal me. I never thought that writing down your feelings and expressing yourself with words could bring so much healing that held you captive for so many years. Satan likes to make you feel ugly, unwanted, dirty, and unworthy every chance he gets. Without Jesus in your life, Satan can take you to dark places that you feel you could never climb out of.

Holding on to the pain of your past and not letting go can really keep you "stuck" in habits, attitudes, and a lifestyle that you never thought you could escape. A little exercise I learned to do to help forgive the person or circumstance of the past was to take two chairs. With the first chair you sit yourself in it. Then you place the other chair facing in front of you, so you are looking at an empty chair. Imagine the person who hurt you in that chair and you talk, yell, scream, cry, or do whatever you need to so that all emotions are being released. Be open and tell the person all your emotional bondage that has been kept stored up for so long. The most important part is to find a way to allow yourself to heal.

During anything that ever happened to you, know that Jesus was with you and was going through the pain and suffering along with you. He never leaves us or forsakes us just like the Bible promises. Look at the cross and that will show you that he has never left you. He knows all struggles and pain of our lives. Remember, he is the author of your life. He has orchestrated everything in your life even when we don't understand why bad things happen to us. We are not to know all, because we are not God. God allows things to happen to us that bring tragedy, triumphs, and tribulations for the growth of our souls. It's hard to accept that, but we must believe that God is always with us and that he never leaves us. He will always take care of us and do what is right for us when he knows when we are ready.

It helps to read the scripture: "Trust in the Lord with all your heart; do not depend on your own understanding. Seek his will in all you do; and he will show you which path to take" (Prov. 3:5–6).

As Adam heard my painful story, he seemed to understand more of what I went through. I could feel a breakthrough for us, and being able to share it all drew me closer to him. He was in silence, but I know deep down God had me talk to him about my story as he had his own story of past hurts that he was dealing with too.

Stopping off in Nevada for the night and playing in the casino for a while was fun. Making new memories with Adam and enjoying a nice big steak dinner felt like we were doing what couples do.

My father-in-law Dan and Kitty had just sold their house and had moved into a new place and needed our help once we arrived.

Helping them move furniture from their storage into their new home, relieved a lot of stress. Being around family and doing things for them made me feel good knowing we had been a part for so long.

The next day, we arrived at Grandma's house to surprise her for the ride of her life. Grandma now was ninety-six years old, sitting in her chair. Adam walked over to her and extended his hand to help her. Seeing that her body was frail, it was hard for her to stand alone.

I never have forgotten what she was wearing, her beautiful blue blouse with dark slacks and wearing a million-dollar smile on her face when she faced her grandson Adam. She always refers Adam to her as "My Adam." Grandma had a hard time walking without her cane but was excited to get into the car.

"I have been waiting a long time for this," she told Adam with excitement on her face. Grandma doesn't smile that often, so seeing her smile made Adam feel like he was fulfilling his promise he made to her so many years ago. Adam gently placed her in the car as I video recorded all the moments. As they drove off, she waved like a little girl happy to finally get the ride she had been waiting for. They were gone not that long, but Adam managed to get the speed of the car over one hundred miles per hour. Grandma loved it all.

After we helped and walked Grandma back into the house, we all had some lunch and talked about so many different things. A few minutes later, I heard, "Come here, dear, I have something for you." She looked over to me motioning me to follow her. I glanced over to Kitty to look for a response from her, but she was just as puzzled as I was. I sat up from the couch and followed her into her bedroom where I found her looking through some boxes in her closet. After she moved two boxes and setting them aside, I was making small talk with her when she handed me a beautiful colorful afghan that she had made.

"Here, I want you to have this, something to remember me by."

With tears in my eyes, I said, "Thank you, I will cherish it and thank you for thinking of me."

"You're special, dear, and I am so happy you are with *my* Adam."

Making me feel even more special, I gave her a hug and told her once again, "Thank you." I thought maybe this was a good-bye as I had seen a vision of her passing about year earlier.

One thing I have learned through this journey that you will hear me repeat more than once is that God's timing is perfect and is always on time. When God shares visions with me, I have had to learn not to try and put a "time" on when things would "come" or "happen" but to know to trust that he is doing everything on his own timing for our good.

After saying good-bye, I couldn't help but think and ask if that was the last time that I would see her alive. I took in every moment and tucked it away deep into my heart.

In talking with Kitty, she shared with me that Grandma never gives any of her items away and that for her to give me the afghan was stating something big about how she felt about me. Even to this day when I wrap up in the afghan for comfort, I think of her and still remember what that day felt like as if it was yesterday.

After getting Dan and Kitty situated and taking care of duties that Adam's parents needed done, it was time to head back home to Colorado. Saying good-bye is never easy but we knew that we would see them soon in Las Vegas that September to celebrate Ash's twenty-fifth birthday.

On the way back home, I expressed to Adam that Shawna was getting baptized later in the month and asked him if it was okay if I surprised her back in Michigan. He agreed to let me go so I could be there to witness such an important event of her life.

I called to let my mom know that I would be coming in for the celebration. I told her to please not to tell Shawna and that I would surprise her at the church, the day of her baptism. My mother assured me that she wouldn't say a word but was pleased that I was coming.

Adam had left the next morning for work. I had put a cute little note in the bottom of his sock without telling him. Trying to find different ways to stay connected to him while we were apart.

The morning of August 22, God woke me up and told me to get rid of the jewelry that Adam had bought for Loren. "Where should I get rid of it all?" I thought at first maybe I should give it to someone. Then I thought maybe to pawn it and get money for it but then I thought, "No, I don't want anyone to wear the jewelry. It needs to be thrown in the trash." I hurriedly got out of bed and went into my drawer where I had placed it all and picked it up and walked it out to the trash. I threw it deep down so that it couldn't be seen.

Seeing that jewelry made me envision her wearing it on her hand and around her neck which made me cringe. The moment I threw it away I saw a flash of Adam asking me for it back. "Why did I just see that? That's weird." I closed the lid and walked back inside.

The feeling was so uncomfortable that I had called Felicia to share with her. We both really didn't know what to think of it, so we just prayed that everything was going to work out.

The weekend came up so quickly to head to Michigan for my big surprise. As I was sitting in the airport waiting to board, God said to me, "You need to erase your book and start over."

"What? Why?" I asked him.

God replied, "Because that was for you and Adam to read not for everyone else. There will be a time you can write your story."

"Hmm. Okay. I will do as you say." Erasing all that I had written and watching over thirty pages disappear in a flash before my eyes, I now was looking at a clean white computer screen. "Now how am I going to start over?"

Feeling discouraged as I sat in my seat on the plane, I bowed my head and asked God to please help me to write this book the way he wanted me to. Once we were in the air and we could have our electronic devices on, I pulled out my computer and to my amazement the words just started pouring out.

I began typing diligently that time flew by so fast and the next thing I heard from the first officer was to put our electronic devices away as we were about to land. I couldn't believe how much I had written in the short two-and-half-hour flight. Rereading what I wrote, I was pleased and couldn't wait to share with my family.

My friend had arranged to pick me up from the airport. Happy to see my friend and being able to catch up with her on her life was nice. When we arrived at our meeting place to meet my mother, I was the one who was surprised. As I was getting out of the car and hugging my mother, she had a smile on her face. She said to me suddenly, "Look in the backseat." With a puzzle look on my face and slowly looking through the window to the back seat, there my sister popped up and said "Surprise!"

"Wait, I am supposed to surprise you!" With us both laughing, Shawna got out of the car so we could hug each other. I had planned on only seeing her the day of her baptism, but her fiancé wouldn't allow her to go all weekend without seeing me, so he sent her to my mother's where she had no choice but to let her know I was in town. Needless to say, he was forgiven.

Before I arrived, I had gone to the Christian bookstore *Mardel* to purchase Shawna her very own first bible and a beautiful cross to hang in her home. I had wrapped it up and couldn't wait to give to her. I went into the bedroom where I was staying and retrieved her gifts from my suitcase to give to her. "Please open this. I was going to give it to you on Sunday, but since you are here, now you can open it." Shawna took the bag from my hand as I video recorded her opening her bible. Her face beamed with happiness and when she saw the cross that was multicolored and beautiful, tears welted in her eyes.

"Thank you, I love it all she said." I told her that having a cross in your home will always keep you close to Jesus and that it reminds you every day on what he did for all of us. Dying and forgiving us for our sins and giving us a new birth and a new life.

I was able to share with my family the start of my book. They enjoyed listening to what I had written so far and encouraged me to keep writing and that my book would help others. Having their support meant a lot to me as I wasn't sure if I really could have the confidence in writing a book.

The day of her baptism was here, and my mother and I were dressed for the occasion. My mother wore a cream blouse with a peach dress coat and a peach skirt to match it. My mother looked beautiful as usual when getting dressed up for any celebrations. With white dress shoes to finish the adding touch to her attire.

I was dressed in a multicolor dress wearing black shoes.

One of my mother's concerns was that Shawna wouldn't be baptized before the passing of my mom's own death and wanted to make sure before she left this earth that both of her daughters were baptized. My mother felt so much relief when my sister told her that she was ready to accept Jesus Christ as her savior. No, my mother is still alive, thank the Lord.

Sitting in the church with my mother, Shawna's fiancé, and his two boys, I was asked to meet Shawna in the room where she was preparing. As I walked into the room, Shawna was slipping on the white robe. I said a prayer to her and thanked the Lord for this time I was able to spend with her and to share this moment that would change her life forever. We shared another hug before leaving the room. I walked back to my seat feeling the anticipation.

As the minister asked Shawna if she had received Jesus Christ as her savior and when Shawna said, "Yes, I claim Jesus Christ as my Savior," my mother and I were holding hands and was happy to see her daughter, my sister being reborn again. We both knew that she would never be the same after this.

Watching herself give her life over to Jesus and being dunked down in the water to kill all her sins and as she was raised to life again, a big chill was felt throughout my body. The Holy Spirit likes to give me a chill when he wants to speak to me and to confirm that this was right, and the spirit was happy. Her baptism was beautiful.

One of the ways I remind myself of my baptism is when I take a shower. While in the shower I get on my hands and knees while the water is pouring down on me and I ask God each morning, "How can I serve you today, Lord? What or who do you want to bring into my life today? I am here to do your work." I then thank him for all my blessings and for all that he is doing in my life. It is a nice reminder that every day you can be baptized again. Remember God sees and knows all. There is no hiding from God so don't be ashamed. He wants you close to him.

The short weekend was lived but in a very spiritual way and now it was time for me to head back home. My family drove me to the airport. On the way, we discussed how Shawna's life just changed and what she could expect. I had downloaded a devotional app onto her phone so that each morning she could start off her day with a scripture to keep her close to Jesus and to keep her spirit growing.

Getting back onto the plane, I felt I had made God proud for doing his work and being a part of my sister's new life. I began to see how God chooses us for different tasks to help others.

Birthday Celebration

It was now fall, September 2017. Big Ashley, Adam, Ash, and I were all meeting Grandpa Dan, and Grandma Kitty in Las Vegas to celebrate Ash's twenty-fifth birthday. Big Ashley had flown into Denver a few days prior to us leaving for Las Vegas. She was unaware who would be waiting for her once we were to arrive.

She hadn't seen her grandparents for years, so we were excited for Big Ashley to have her own surprise. Before Adam came home, I asked him one morning, "Did you find something from me in your suitcase?"

"What are you talking about?" he asked.

"I hid something for you," I stated.

"No, I didn't see anything, where should I look?"

"You will find it." Not telling him where it was.

Later that day, he kept bugging me and kept asking me where I had hidden it. I played along with him and wouldn't respond. He later called me and demanded me to tell him where it was. With his disturbing attitude I was receiving on the line, the game was over and wasn't fun anymore. Finally telling him to look in one of his socks.

"There you happy now?" I asked sarcastically.

"Yes, thank you," was his reply.

Adam had arrived back home a few short days before our trip. While I was in our bedroom, he came walking in and asked, "What did you do with that jewelry?" Looking at him in shock and surprised that he asked, and wondering why he cared about the jewelry, "I threw it away!"

"Why would you do that? That was good jewelry," he barked back at me.

"Why does it matter what I did with it? It's gone."

"You just threw good jewelry away."

"You told me I could do whatever I wanted with it, so I did."

Ending that conversation quick, I left the room and went into the garage.

Adam had followed me out there to get into his truck when he started showing me something on his phone. Suddenly a picture of Loren's hand appeared with the ring on her finger. She made some comment about seeing the ring for the last time on her hand in her message. I asked Adam why he still had her number in his phone. With no response from him, I asked and made him delete it in front of me. I was so angry that I went into the house.

"God, what is going on? Why is she still here?"

God kept repeating, "He's not coming back the same. You will see a new man soon. He's happy you stayed." Not understanding and feeling like the nightmare wasn't over but just begun again.

With the fear inside of me and afraid of losing him, I just let it go and started thinking about our trip with the family and having God next to me. I kept in the faith and couldn't wait to see this new man very soon.

While sitting in the Denver airport waiting to board our plane to Las Vegas, I spoke to Big Ashley and told her what had happened with the jewelry incident. She was concerned that her dad was playing games again with me when she decided to go onto Facebook and look at Loren's profile. She could see that her father and Loren weren't friends but what she did see was she still had a picture of my dog Gracee on her page.

"That's strange, why would she keep that on her page?" Ashley wondered.

I found myself in so much fear once again and knew something wasn't right. Big Ashley told me not to worry about it and that she would keep an eye out for me.

Arriving into Las Vegas with Big Ashley still not knowing that her grandparents were waiting for us, we got off the plane. Adam was keeping us distracted until he had seen his parents' truck waiting for us. Big Ashley kept looking around asking us why we were just walking in circles when she noticed her grandparents' truck. She and everyone else were so happy and excited to see each other. It had been years since they saw one another, so seeing the reunion was a blessing.

During the time in Vegas, Ash had been playing with the idea of getting a tattoo but was scared. Finally, after Big Ashley and she contemplated, she decided to get her first tattoo. Big Ashley and Ash had decided on tattooing little hearts on their pinky fingers. Seeing Ash sitting in the chair holding a towel close to her face, you could see the fear in her eyes. I wasn't too sure if she was going to go through with it. We all cheered her on with our support. I don't have any tattoos so I couldn't relate to the pain or anything but just seeing the look on Ash's face was enough for me to know that I wouldn't be getting any tattoos in my future.

We had decided to see a magic show. With all of us dressed up and looking sharp, I wanted to take pictures to share with family and friends on Facebook. Adam was reluctant of taking any photos with me or even posting anything about us. In fact, anytime I tried tagging him any photo, a message would pop up that he had to approve it. That was very frustrating, and I felt again he was hiding me. Even with the signs I was feeling from Adam, he still seemed like he wanted to be present with me. He was loving to me and not rude, so I just thought maybe I was making too much out of nothing.

We had our last dinner to celebrate Ash before our trip was over. Big Ashley and Ash had a lot of fun playing in the casinos. They made their own fun memories while Adam and I made ours.

During dinner, we all talked about when the next time we would be able to get together again. I suggested that everyone to come to Colorado for Christmas so that Owen our other grandson could see his grandparents too. Living so far away doesn't really allow Kitty and Dan to see their grandson all that often. Everyone seemed to be excited and was looking forward to yet another reunion.

After we returned home, I continued writing my book. God kept saying, "Finish your book. Finish your book." I had only been writing for about two weeks, but God was determined on getting me to finish my book.

Adam had left a couple days later to head back to work. The salon was in slow season, so I took my computer with me to write. As I would write in my book there were times that I couldn't even remember what I had written as God was leading me where he needed me to go in the book and with his words. Satan tried to get me to stop writing. I became stuck. I called my mom and said, "I can't write anymore," crying out to her.

"What do you mean, Heather?" she asked.

"I don't know it's like I am blocked," I said. She told me to leave it for a bit and then to come back. Whenever I tried to stop typing God would say, "Finish your book." With feeling like I couldn't, I went into our tanning room and began kneeling against the chair and prayed for Satan to go away and that I needed to finish this book because I was doing God's work. I asked for Jesus to get Satan out of my head and to give me the words to finish. When looking up, I had this burst of energy and went back to my desk and finished the book.

It was now September 27, 2017, Adam had come home, and I was anxious to share with him my book. "Do you want to read it before I send it off?" I asked him.

"No, I already know what it says. I lived it. I am the star of the book," he responded sarcastically.

"Well, that hurts, I thought you would want to read it before I send it out. It's raw and real. Are you sure?" I asked one more time thinking he would change his mind.

"No, just send it," were his final words.

"Okay, here it goes." I pushed the SEND button to the publisher without knowing if they would accept my book or even want to publish it.

That night lying in bed, I started hearing, "They want your book *The Voice of Faith* in production." I started seeing a vision of my book on our shelves in our tanning salons. Seeing that vision made me very excited. "Is this really going to happen?" in asking God. Then he showed me the cover and the book started floating around in the room once again.

Premiere of the Book

It was now Sunday October 1, 2017. Adam and I were standing in church singing when I started hearing once again, "*The Voice of Faith* in production, *The Voice of Faith* begins." I kept hearing it throughout the service. I couldn't help but smile and get excited.

After church, I kept sharing with Adam what I had been hearing all day. I don't know what he was thinking, but I knew exactly what I was hearing throughout the day and into the night. It was hard to focus on anything but my book.

Waking up the next morning on our anniversary, October 2, 2017, Adam and I were preparing to take a drive to Blackhawk to celebrate our special day. As we were driving toward Denver, I started seeing confetti floating in our car. "Adam, I am seeing confetti in our car. I feel like they are going to call me today," I said with high anticipation.

"Don't get too far ahead of yourself now," he said, chuckling.

The car began to feel very heavy with confetti and my book still floating around. Within twenty minutes, my cell phone rang. I could see it was the publisher.

"This is it. They are calling," I said as I looked at Adam.

"Answer it!" he said.

As he was holding my hand, I answered it, "Hello."

"Is this Heather Larribas?" the man asked me.

"Yes, this is she."

The man said, "You submitted a book called the *Voice of Faith* a few days ago, and I am happy to say that we would like to publish your book."

"Are you serious?" I asked, not believing what my ears were hearing.

"Yes, we would be honored to publish your book," the man reassured me.

Adam had grabbed my hand and said, "Congratulations, good job." Feeling with excitement running through my body, the man gave me more details what to expect in the upcoming days.

He had told me that a woman was my publisher and it would take about six to eight months to get my book published and their company was out of Meadville, PA. Right away, I remember the day God told me in July about my book. Everything he said came true and then when I realized it was on my anniversary that the news was shared, I then realized why God had told me to finish my book every day. He knew exactly when they were going to call me. I tried explaining to Adam that he had told me all of this in July, but as always, Adam never really believed me that God had given me this special gift. God also reminded me that years ago he had told me that Adam would be part of my book and then he said, "Adam, PA." It all makes sense now. Adam was the one who gave me the publisher. God was trying to get his attention that day Adam found the publisher on the television screen.

God is always working for us and wanting to get our attention if we would just stop and listen or recognize the signs. I couldn't contain myself any longer. I had to call everyone to let them know that I was now an author and that my book was accepted. I called Felicia, my mom, my mother-in-law, my sister, and my children. They were all excited for me and couldn't believe my book was accepted.

My day was filled with so much joy and full of blessings. When we arrived at the hotel and was checking in, I began telling the clerk that it was our anniversary and that I had just found out moments earlier that my book was accepted and being published. The lady was so happy for me that she upgraded our room to a suite at no additional cost to us. The blessings just kept pouring in. This was God's victory, not mine, but he was shining the spotlight on me letting me know he was proud.

Walking into our suite with our bags, I noticed the beautiful room. When looking out from all the windows, seeing snow-capped mountains was breathtaking view from the top floor of our suite. The room had a luxury bathroom, a living room, a king-size bed, and a hot tub that overlooked the mountains.

After putting our things away, we went back downstairs to have dinner and play in the casino. Walking around, holding hands, we watched other players play. Enjoying our time and winning a little here and there without gambling too much. It was getting late, so we decided to head back up to our room.

While we were basking in the hot tub with bubbles over flowing around us and soft candles lit around the edge, Adam and I began to talk. It seemed he was more comfortable with me, so I wanted to talk about us since I was feeling things were still distant between us. I needed to know where we stood and if this was what he wanted. He assured me that he did want to be back home, which eased my mind. Still not feeling confident, I had to trust his words.

We had discussed about our situation with our tanning salons and finances. He had mentioned that he thought maybe he would be getting laid off in November until January. Reassuring him that we would get through this all, I would start to pay our monthly bills ahead for the time if it was to happen that we would be still financially stable.

I couldn't help but be upset with all the money that was lost from that year while he was away. I had still been paying on the third location, rent, and taxes from the previous year. We were still waiting for another tenant to take over the lease. It was still our responsibility until the new tenant took ownership of the space.

I knew God would provide for us no matter what and I kept the faith that I was doing what he instructed me to do. Closing the third location was the best decision that was made to help us sustain our other two salons.

Adam and I seemed to be on the same page on how we were going to fix our finances and he made me feel secure in us, so I didn't bring up anymore of my fears. There were many times I would feel Loren around me or sometimes her face would float close into my mind making me think she was still around.

As we got out of the hot tub, climbing into bed, I wanted to be close and to celebrate fourteen years of our marriage. Knowing that it hadn't been easy for a long time, I wanted a brand-new start. I had told him that we need to do things different and spend more time together. We both knew though we would have to be a part as we still had so many bills to pay.

Waking up the next morning, we packed up and headed back home. On the way, we talked more about my book and I asked him again if he would like to read it, but he still said he didn't need to and that he was okay with all that I had written.

Adam and I were having lunch one afternoon when the news broke out about the hurricane that was about to hit where our daughter Big Ashley lived. In fear, we called her up and purchased her a plane ticket to come to Colorado for safety. Seeing Adam so concerned and wanting to keep his family safe made me feel that he was really investing in all of us. Big Ashley had to leave her son Owen who was with his dad and step-mom in Tennessee and her boyfriend.

Big Ashley stayed with us for about two weeks until the storm passed, and it was safe for her to return home. Having Big Ashley with us was nice. She played with the boys and helped around the house and the salons.

In talking to Big Ashley, God started showing me that after this storm I saw her getting closer to her boyfriend so much that I felt like they were inseparable. God kept telling me that her life was about to change and that she would see it come very soon and she would be happy. Ashley was ready for a change in her life since she had been dating her boyfriend for quite some time.

Adam had returned to work and I returned to the salons. My book was now underway of being published. All the necessary documents were signed, and it was out of my hands and into God's.

It was a Saturday night late in October when I was lying in bed watching television when suddenly, I heard Adam's voice in my head. "Please forgive me for what I am about to do." Not really paying attention to it, his voice became louder. After about three times of hearing it, I realized what I was hearing, and this dark feeling came over me. "What is going on? Why do I feel like he is seeing her again?" With the urge to look at our bank account, I noticed he had just spent money in a town that he needed not to be in, and it looked as if it was for two people having dinner. I called my mom out of anger and fear and she told me to ask him about it.

"You have every right to ask him, Heather. Don't be afraid," she told me.

"I don't understand why he came back if he is still seeing her or why did God have me write this book?" I questioned to my mom. "I believe God. I know he's doing something for us but what?"

"I don't know, Heather. I can't hear God like you can or see the visions that you see. You must trust God."

After talking to her, I hung up and tried to call Adam. Of course, not getting an answer and going straight to voice mail, the pit of my stomach fell to the ground. "I know he is still seeing her. I can feel it. What am I doing?" Crying out to God and asking him what he wanted me to do, he began to show me a Christmas tree with a white box that Adam was handing me. God kept repeating the same things to me, "He's not coming back the same. He's happy you stayed," he then added. "Two peas in a pod and he showed Adam in the white robe with a cross on it as if he was really following Jesus."

The visions and the words that God gave me made me calm and settled me down. They seemed to be the same visions I had seen earlier in the year which led me to believe not all my visions I had been shown had come true yet. I still would see the vision of me turning Adam away but not understanding how or when as my arms were wide open for him when he returned in July.

Trying to get some sleep after all of that was hard. Earlier the next morning, Adam had called me and made up some lame excuse that he didn't hear his phone. We got into a heated argument, and not wanting it to get worse knowing he was on his way home, I stopped the conversation. He told me that he didn't want to be under a microscope every time he was to leave and that he wasn't going to live that way. I agreed too. I didn't want to feel like I had to check up on my husband. When I questioned him about the charges, he got angry and hung up on me, which confirmed it was true.

I didn't call him back as I had nothing to say. A few hours later well into the night, Adam texted me and said, "Holy crap, I about hit a bear!" Once he said that, God reminded me of another vision he had given me long ago about Adam almost hitting something and that it stopped him in his tracks.

"Maybe this is it, maybe he has had his moment now and now he will come back a new man."

I responded, asking him if he was okay and his reply was yes but just shaken up a little.

He had shared with me he would have one more rotation then would be laid off for the rest of the year. Feeling relief knowing he would be home with me for the next six to eight weeks gave me peace.

Earlier in the previous months when Adam returned, he had bought a white pick-up truck to drive back and forth to save on miles from using his other truck. Another journal entry I had written years ago seeing Adam buying a white-and-maroon truck.

God perfectly places things, people, and circumstances in our lives when he knows when it will be needed. Since he was getting laid off, he had decided to sell the truck to help with our finances. I had called Felicia and told her about my fear of not having enough money and asked her to pray for us and our finances. A few days later, she called me back to let me know that Paul, her husband, was interested in buying the truck.

"Seriously, you are?"

"Yes, he wants to drive that rather than his new BMW in the snow," she explained to me.

"Oh my gosh, that is wonderful, thank you so much."

The money allowed us to pay our bills ahead more for the rest of the year giving me relief since Adam would be home. I tried sharing with Adam on how God orchestrated this all. I have a bad habit in trying to get Adam to believe that God is real, and it has been so important for me for him to believe me. I now realize that God will work with each one of us on his own time and he will allow us to go down the paths that we need before he steps in and changes our direction.

THANKSGIVING

IT WAS NOW NOVEMBER 2017 AND THE holidays were right around the corner. Knowing that Adam was on his last rotation, I was getting excited for our family to be around. The year before was very gloomy, reminding me that Adam had left again, leaving just Ash, Eastyn, Brystyn, and myself to celebrate alone.

About a week later, the realtor who was helping us with the other tanning salon called to give me an update. He felt that he would have new owners taking over the space soon. I was feeling optimistic about everything and finally seeing a light at the end of the tunnel.

To pass the time, Ash had bought her and me a ticket to see the Denver Broncos and the New England Patriots play a game. The day of the game was extremely cold and frigid. Ash and I were bundled up in Patriot gear, not letting the cold get in the way of watching her favorite team. We took lots of pictures and video recorded some of the game. Ash was happy that the Patriots won. "It was worth sitting in the cold, Mom," she said as we walked to our car after the game. Hugging her, I told her that it was nice to have had this time with her, making a great memory.

The morning after the game, I was cleaning the bathroom when God said, "I am reversing everything."

"What do you mean, God?" I asked.

He then showed me a huge blender in the bathroom, and he started putting in all the women, including Loren, the third tanning salon, our home, and all the debt. Then he started blending it up. Watching it being poured out, it was like a white milkshake that looked pure, soft, and new. It even felt like a new beginning and that all bad things and feelings were finally gone.

He even put in the man who hurt Adam when he was a child and told me that Adam was a new man and ready to do the work. He was ready to save our marriage. The vision was so strong, and it held so much definition to me that I couldn't forget it.

Adam's Grandma was on the outside of the blender as if she was looking into it and seeing all the changes. I am not sure what she had to do with it, but knowing God, I know that he knows and would reveal when the time was right.

With another vision coming along right after seeing the blender, I was seeing Adam on the outside of my door to an apartment knocking and asking to come in. As I opened the door, Adam was looking at me with a sorrow look upon his face like as if he was about to cry. The feeling I felt when seeing him was like it had been a long time since we saw each other, and I didn't know how I felt about him. Hearing the words "back in a flash!" God shouted to me. The feeling along with the vision as I opened the door felt like it was a cold winter evening. Then God spoke again and said, "December." I started thinking it was coming soon since December was near. I couldn't understand why I was in an apartment seeing that we were living in our dream home.

I was overwhelmed with what was being shown to me that I wrote it all down in my journal. As I was writing, God shared with me and told me that Ash was going to be pregnant and that one of our girls would be pregnant by the time a wedding came. "A wedding?" I pondered. "Which one of our children is going to get married?" None of our children were engaged at that time. I went back to November 11, 2016 entry of my journal and wrote down "wedding bells," "a baby," and "a funeral." "That's a weird combination," I thought.

Later that day, God started showing me the date December second. The number kept floating around in the air. "Hmm I wonder if it's this December or next December?"

More visions were coming with each passing day that I couldn't ignore. I kept seeing Adam and his parents around a table and I could see and feel so many emotions. At one point, I saw Adam crying and telling everyone he was sorry for how he treated us all. I saw Dan, Kitty, and myself all hugging each other. God kept floating around the Christmas tree and the white box. "Something is going to happen. I just know it. I can feel it. It's getting close."

A few days later, Adam was on his way home for the rest of the year. I started preparing for Thanksgiving. It was a relief to know that he would be here and that he wouldn't be getting any calls to go back to work until the first of the year. We had asked our friends Felicia and Paul to join us.

On Thanksgiving Day, I shared with Felicia all the visions that were coming to me and when I mentioned that Ash was going to be pregnant, she instantly got a bad feeling. One of Felicia's gift from God was that she could feel things, something that I quite didn't have so intensely like her. She knew something wasn't right, but she didn't know when this would take place.

In changing the subject, Felicia shared that she and Paul had been thinking about building another house. I started seeing visions of the house being build and then not being built. It felt like it was going to be very rocky for the two of them during the process. I also saw Paul working from home and he was very happy. Sharing with Felicia what I saw for Paul, she was so happy and excited for this change.

I would continue sharing with Felicia all that God was sharing with me and each time she would assure me that God was sharing with her that Adam and I wouldn't divorce. She could see that Adam was struggling and that something didn't feel right to her too. When she would look at Adam, she could feel his burden that he was carrying.

Adam, Ash, Eastyn, Brystyn, Felicia, and Paul, all sat down and enjoyed the Thanksgiving feast. Adam cooked his famous deep-fried turkey along with serving green bean casserole, devil eggs, cranberry sauce, mash potatoes, stuffing, and gravy. We all ate until our stomachs were about to explode, topping it off with deserts. It was a good day sharing with family and friends.

With Adam having so much time off from work, he started helping in the salons, reminding me on how we started all those years ago working together as a team. We were rebuilding our business and spending more time together. "Is this what you were showing me, God? Is this how you are reversing everything?" I waited for God to respond but he was quiet.

FAMILY REUNION

ON A SNOWY DECEMBER DAY, ADAM WAS getting our home ready for Christmas. He decorated the outside edge of our home with lights in the front and in the back using Christmas reflectors making it look very festive. He even went so far as to get a big Santa Clause blow-up balloon who was sitting on a chair holding presents with the elves. He placed it out in our front yard. It was so big you could see it from a distance when driving into our neighborhood.

Ash and I were decorating inside the home. She and I always enjoyed decorating and putting up the tree while listening and singing to Christmas carols. She placed garland around the stair case, adding ribbons on the handles of the cupboards in the kitchen. I was putting decorative towels in each bathroom, and Eastyn was placing window decals on the sliding glass door.

As we were finishing dressing the Christmas tree, Adam came walking in.

"Would you do the honor and putting the angel top on the tree?" I asked him.

"Sure," he said.

Getting the ladder from the garage and placing by the eight-foot tree, he climbed up and added the finishing touch. I video recorded it and savored the moment. It felt like Christmas was going to be warm and loving. In the moments of all that was occurring, I was thanking God for all that he was doing and the blessings he was giving me.

It's easy to take God for granted when we all get used to things in our lives. He is the one who gives us all that we have, and it is our duty to be grateful and to thank him continuously. He is the one who has given us the skills and talents. All he asks in return is to believe and to follow him and to let him be in our lives every day. Is that asking too much from the one who breathed life in you and died for you? I didn't think so.

One morning while we were eating breakfast, I looked up and around Adam was his grandma. She was so strong and making me feel like as if she wanted to talk to him.

"Adam, I don't know what this means but your grandma is really close to you. I see her, I feel like you need to call her." Her birthday was drawing near so I thought maybe she had something to say to him.

Adam's response was, "Okay, I will give her a call." I finished up breakfast, brushed my teeth, and was headed out the door to another day in the salon.

In getting home that night, I had went to the mailbox to retrieve our mail. Thumbing through the mail, I came across a card from his grandma. "This is interesting, just this morning I saw her around Adam and now I am holding a card from her. Is there message here God?" I asked.

Walking in the door and finding Adam in our room, I showed him the card. "Did you call her today?" in asking him. "Yes, we had a nice talk. She was asking if we had received her card yet, but I told her I didn't know. She had been sick for a few days and she thought maybe she was going to die. She had been in the hospital due to her heart condition."

"See, Adam, I knew there was a reason she was around you. You are so special to her and she wanted to talk to you. Can't you see now why God showed me her to you this morning?"

Adam just looked at me and said, "I guess."

I was thinking, "What more does he need to see? It's hitting him right in the face but still won't acknowledge it?"

The days were drawing near for everyone to fly in to celebrate Christmas. Big Ashley and Owen arrived a day earlier than Dan and Kitty. They were due in on Christmas Eve.

The family went to the Christmas Eve service to the church I had been attending for the last two years. The best part of the service was in the end when we all sang "Holy Night." Seeing everyone holding lighted candles throughout the dark room reminded us of the night when our Savior Jesus Christ was born. The room was filled with the Holy Spirit and feeling peace everywhere.

Big Ashley, Ash, and the boys all went home while Adam and I headed to the airport to pick up his parents. Their plane was on time which made getting their luggage easy and soon we were back in the car heading home to open presents to celebrate Christmas. Adam's tradition with his family was on Christmas Eve presents were exchanged, and on Christmas morning, we would attend a Catholic Mass.

Excited to see everyone including Daxx, his girlfriend, and her daughter, we were all ready to get the party started. Earlier that month, Adam and I sat down together and wrote our traditional Christmas letter and we read it aloud. It reminded me of when we sat down to write it. Adam was holding my hand while I wrote and while he spoke. His letter was heartfelt to the family and it was very convincing that Adam was home for good.

Listening to all the Christmas letters showed me even though our family had been broken for years, that the tradition kept on and the kids were excited to read their letters. Hearing the first Christmas letter from Owen who now was ten years was added to the bunch.

Each one of the kids, grandchildren, and our parents started opening their gifts. Seeing their faces light up and happy with their treasures gave me a sense that things in our family was headed in the right direction. Adam had gone and bought his mom a beautiful cross necklace. The look on his mother's face showed she was very humbled to see that she received such a gift like that from her son. Little moments like that I just stopped and thanked God for all the work he was doing in our lives.

When I opened the card from Adam from my stocking and began reading it, I felt something in that moment changed my mood. I reread what he wrote about enjoying the family and making the most of it. I had a surge of heat go through my body telling me that things wouldn't be the same next Christmas. Trying to shake that feeling wasn't easy. Looking over at Adam I could see he was in the moments with his family but not really me. Not saying a word to anyone but keeping a smile on my face.

After all the presents were opened, I noticed that the white box that God kept showing me was nowhere to be found. Doubt started creeping in and I knew Satan was getting into my head. I went into our bathroom to get away from everyone to catch my breath. Looking into the mirror, "God I don't understand. What are you trying to say to me? Where is the white box you keep showing me?" I was crying out to him.

Waking up the next morning to Christmas, Adam said to me as we were lying in bed, "I forgot one more Christmas present for you. It's in my dresser drawer. Get it." Jumping out of bed in hopes thinking maybe it was the white box, I went over to his dresser drawer and opened the second drawer. Inside a white bag, I pulled out the white box! "There it is. I knew God was showing me this all along." I shared with Adam what God had showed me for a couple of months and was pleased that once again God always follows through with his promises.

The white box consisted of a pen that said *Diamonds of Silk*. It was a cosmetic pen to help with my discouraging wrinkles around my eyes and forehead. He had heard me complain about it and thought maybe it would help. I have realized the wrinkles on my forehead is because I think too much and always making a facial expression to exuberate the wrinkles.

Seeing the box made me trust God even more even though I knew things weren't right in my life. I kept my eyes on him and listened for his direction when he would speak to me.

After church service, we all came back and enjoyed the holiday with a Christmas dinner. While everyone was talking, Kitty shared with me that years before, a woman had approached her telling her that she had a message for her from God. Kitty was told by that woman that someone in her family would be writing books and their name would be well-known. She also stated that the books would be about forgiveness, infidelity, and repentance. Listening to her, God said, "You are breaking the curse." I thought the books that Kitty was talking about were the journals that I had written but now I know it is the books that I am writing.

Big Ashley and Owen had a short stay with us, as she had to get back to work and Owen had to get back to his dad to celebrate with him. We enjoyed the time with them, but it was time to say goodbye. We all drove them up to the airport.

A couple of days later after I returned from work, Adam suggested to his parents that we all head up to Blackhawk to play in the casino. Adam's parents enjoy playing penny Keno and with the time they were here, we wanted to make it fun.

On our way up to the casino, Adam stopped off to a fast-food place. Kitty and I were in the backseat while Adam and Dan were in the front. We were having good conversation when she and I noticed the worker was taking his sweet time in taking our order. We were all getting frustrated that comments were made that was irritating Adam. When we finally ordered and pulled up to get our food, I had rolled down my window and made a comment to the guy when he responded back to me that he had a rough night and was sorry for the delay.

The food order was all wrong but all of us could see Adam getting madder, especially after I gave the guy my choice of words to him after he said he had a long night. Kitty didn't say much except that her order was wrong too.

Adam peeled out of the drive-thru and then he drove to another drive-thru to get his food. I and Kitty looked at each other and couldn't understand why he was getting so mad. We tried talking to Adam, and when his mom said something Adam didn't like, he blew up on us all. Then his dad jumped in and told Adam not to speak to his mother that way and that he was tired of the way he had been treating all of us including me. Well, that set Adam off even more. He got his food from the lady and drove off.

Instead of driving toward Denver, Adam whipped the car around and started heading back home. He was driving fast and reckless. Words were said back and forth between his dad and Adam. In the heated moment, Dan said that he and his mom were going to leave and take an earlier flight out. I then chimed in and pleaded with Adam to stop talking to his dad the way he was and to turn around so we could enjoy the day.

Adam continued to drive to our house ignoring us all, so Kitty and I just sat back and didn't say another word. As he pulled us into the driveway and opened the garage, Dan and Kitty got out of the car and headed into the house to get their things. Adam didn't say one word to me as he got out of the car but slammed the door in my face, leaving me locked out of the house. I banged on the door, but no one came out, so I waited for a few minutes and then knocked again. Kitty opened the door for me, and I walked in. As I was entering the kitchen, I saw Adam in a huddle with his dad by the kitchen table. When he saw me, he reached his arms out for me. "I am so sorry, angel. Please forgive me."

Looking at him, I asked, "Where is this coming from?"

But his mom just said, "Don't worry about it. He's asked to be forgiven and that is all that matters."

Not saying a word, I hugged Adam tightly and his parents. Emotions were so high in all of us that once we calmed down, we got back into the car and headed back toward Denver.

It was quiet along the way, which allowed me to talk to God. I had remembered all that he showed me in a vision regarding his parents around a table. I thought that was the moment Adam would finally have his repentance about all that he had done to everyone. Feeling like all that God had showed me through the last couple years had ended. "Now is this the time for a new beginning?" I asked myself.

Arriving to the casino, we sat down to dinner since none of us ate any of the food we had bought earlier. Everyone was in better spirits. Things were back to normal and we were talking and laughing. After dinner, Dan and Kitty went to play their games while Adam and I went our way. Walking through the casino, he kept me close to his side. Watching him win at Black Jack and cheering him on, I was feeling relieved. After a few hours, well late into the night, we decided to head back home. It had been a long day, and everyone was tired.

The next day was New Year's Eve Day. Adam was packing to leave to head back to work. I had noticed in November after returning from his last rotation when placing his keys on the dresser, there was a key that looked like a house key. When asking him about it, he told me it was a key to the man camp. I don't know why I thought of it right then and there, but I did, and it made me very uncomfortable. I didn't want to see him leave as I was used to him being there all the time.

He went out to the kitchen where his parents were and hugged them and said goodbye. I walked him out to his truck and while I was hugging him, I wished him a Happy New Year and that we would make 2018 the best year yet. "I love you," he said to me. "I will see you in a couple of weeks."

I went back in and Kitty and I started talking about everything that had happened and what she had observed. "I can see that he is really trying but in order for your marriage to work, it needs to be just the two of you." At the time, Ash and her boys were still living with us. Ash wanted to get on her own and I knew it was time that she did.

Kitty had noticed at times Adam would just be sitting in a chair, but not really being here presently. She thought all the chaos in our home was too much for him. When she told me that, I felt so much fear and instantly I was afraid of losing my husband and my marriage. I thought about all that she had said that day and was really seeing that changes needed to be made.

Ash was twenty-five and it was time that she was on her own being able to raise her two boys by herself.

Appreciating the honesty from Kitty and her telling me what she observed, I started putting a plan together in my head.

Ash and I were sitting watching television. As the ball fell to ring in the New Year "2018," I had this overwhelming feeling and stood up and God shouted out, *"It's all over. It's a new beginning. She's gone, and your husband is back for good. He never wants to lose you again. He's so sorry for all that he has put you through. You will see a changed man. He's not coming back the same."* Hearing so much from God as he kept repeating the same things to me completely puzzled me. "Why is he talking about Loren? She's gone now. It's just me and Adam."

I thought when God told me that it was over it was meant that Ash and I were over and that she would be moving out soon. Just as I thought that, I saw a vision of Ash in a new apartment and Eastyn was showing me his room. I ignored the other things that God said to me and only focused on Ash.

I called Adam while he was driving once again to wish him a Happy New Year. I also told him that I was wanting a fresh New Year to start with just him and me. I presented the idea of Ash getting her own apartment so when he came home it would just be the two of us.

I thought I would have received a better response from him but all he said was, "Okay." I could tell that he didn't want to talk much so I ended our conversation and told him to drive safe.

A New Beginning

WAKING UP TO A NEW YEAR THE next morning was a good feeling. I couldn't help but think about all the anticipation of what the year was going to bring. Knowing that God was on my side, I knew that no matter what he oversaw my life and that I needed to obey him and listen for his direction.

Ask yourself this, wouldn't it be nice to know that none of us would have to worry or wonder about our lives if we would just trust God? What would your lives look like? I bet there would be less worry, less stress, less illnesses, less relationships broken if we would just surrender to him.

Being in the human flesh, we are so afraid of letting go of our own control. We continue to get in the way of God's work which hinders us, and we end up going down different paths, only thinking of ourselves. We become lost and we forget to listen to the only voice of our good shepherd. We listen to other sheep and we become lost.

"But you don't believe me because you are not my sheep. My sheep listen to my voice; I know them, and they follow me. I give them eternal life, and they will never perish. No one can snatch them away from me" (John 10:26–28).

Reading that scripture helps to keep me alert and to only listen for the voice of God. God always lets me know it's him when he shares by adding "in the name of Jesus," which gives me no doubt that I am hearing God. We all have our own special relationship with him. He will speak to you in a way that he only knows how to get your attention. Take the time and ask him how he wants to communicate with you. Allow yourself to get to know him. Remember he created you, so he knows every hair on your head.

Walking out to the kitchen to find Kitty sitting at the table, I shared with her the conversation that I had with Ash the night before. Feeling at peace with the decision to help Ash in getting herself an apartment, I thanked her again for talking to me. Kitty was happy to hear that changes were being made and that I wasn't wasting any time and started to make things happen. I knew it was the right thing to do.

Dan and Kitty spent their last day with Daxx and his girlfriend. Ash and I took down all the decorations and put them away for another year while reminiscing about the holidays. We were happy to get our home looking back to normal. We left the outside decorations up for Adam to take down upon his return. He had taken down the Santa Claus balloon before he left just leaving the lights on the house.

Ash was getting excited about moving, so we started going through all her things. Looking at all the baby stuff she had acquired she decided to get rid of. "It's not like I am going to have another kid, Mom. I don't need all this stuff," Ash said as she was looking at it all.

"You never know it might come in handy," I stated back.

Piling up a basinet, a changing table, a crib, a bathtub, a bouncer, storage bins that contained clothes of all different sizes from newborn to toddler, and toys that were for babies were now placed in her car and we were headed to Goodwill. Knowing that someone else could make good use out of all the nice furniture and clothing she had.

Getting back from dropping things off, Ash could now get a clear picture of all she had and needed for a new apartment.

The next few days we went to look at apartments. While driving to other apartments, God said, "Pine Bluffs and Champions." Wondering if that was where he wanted her to go, we called and went to both places. Champions was a little too expensive, but Pine Bluffs was more in her budget. Her move in date was scheduled February 8, just in time for my mother to arrive to help us all.

I attended both salons while Adam was away working. To keep the line of communication open between us, he would call me daily after he was off talking with me for over an hour. Sharing with him of all the changes that were about to take place the next time he was off, he seemed happy for Ash and the boys.

Some nights after I closed, I would try to call him to say one last good night, but his phone would either go to voice mail or he wouldn't answer putting me in an emotional tailspin. "Why can't he answer? I hate this, not this again," were the thoughts that would go through my mind and not being able to sleep at night.

Still knowing we were rebuilding, and it was a new year, I didn't say anything to him about how I was feeling. I will admit I was still weak when it came to him and afraid to speak up. I kept asking God to give me more strength. He would assure me that things would be new and better soon.

It was now time for Adam to return for his days off. Ash and I had been packing all month and buying things to get her ready for her new life and her new beginning on her own. Ash had never lived on her own, so this was a big step for her, and I was so proud. She had always lived with either my mother, boyfriends, or with us, so this was huge to make such a change.

As Adam walked into our room with his red suitcase and tossing his keys onto the dresser, I was relieved seeing him and his things. He walked over to me and hugged and gave me a kiss.

He had left the room when I walked over to the dresser, and looking at his keys, I noticed that one key that he said was to the man camp was now off his key ring. "Why is that gone?" Immediately I asked myself. Then I thought well maybe he finally gave back the key to Loren. I didn't know for sure the truth, but Satan was really messing with me and putting all these doubts and fears into my head. "Stop this, Heather. Adam is back for good." I was putting myself through so much worry, but something just didn't feel right. Even when Adam would hug me or kiss me, it didn't feel sincere. It seemed once again I was the one always trying to get his attention in every way.

During the time Adam was home, we received a phone call from the realtor that there was a tenant who agreed to take over the third location. The only downfall to that was the new tenant wouldn't be taking possession until July which meant that we still had to pay the rent until then. Frustrated that we were still obligated for seven more months but at the same time seeing that it was all going to end still gave us relief.

HEART OF LOVE

FEBRUARY CAME FAST. KNOWING THE MONTH OF February brings the famous Super Bowl game, Ground Hog Day, Presidents Day, and the holiday of love, Valentine's Day.

Ash was so bummed to see her team New England Patriots lose the title to the Eagles. That night we watched the game was stressful. She was yelling and screaming at the television as she watched her team walk away without the trophy. "This sucks," she says, "I am so mad."

With the team losing confused me too, because earlier in the months, God had said that they would win, and he had showed me Tom Brady with a sixth Super Bowl ring. Once again, I had to remind myself that it's God's timing on everything and just because he shows me things doesn't always mean it's going to happen at that exact same time that I think it should. "Maybe the vision is for next year, Ashley, I don't know. I am not God. I just know what he showed me. I am sorry your team lost," is all I could say.

My mother arrived a day before her birthday. Seeing my mother was a relief. The feelings of uneasiness were building up more each day so having her here to talk with me helped me to stay in the faith. Her birthday was spent helping us move Ash into her apartment. She watched the boys while Daxx, his girlfriend, Ash, and I moved all the furniture and boxes in.

Ash and my mom spent the next day's unpacking boxes. My mom took her shopping for kitchen necessities. Seeing her new place decorated and the boys enjoying their own space and excited to show me their room made me realize even more that this was long overdue, and it was nice seeing everyone happy.

"Now maybe I can be happy with Adam and just myself. We never really had anytime by ourselves to be just us in our home." Looking forward to the day he was to return so we could celebrate Valentine's Day and without Ash and the boys living with us.

I was trying to decide on what to get him for Valentine's Day. Being creative, I came up with something I never did before. A year ago, I had bought a jar of date night cards that I never was able to give him. Recalling back to that time when he had decided to leave our marriage again. I wanted to make this year special, so I went and bought a huge card that said "I LOVE YOU."

Opening the card up, I taped all the little date night cards throughout the card and thought when Adam was home on his days off, we could pick out a card and do what it said to do. There were all kinds of different dates that wouldn't cost a lot of money but would make good memories and allow us to have fun and get to know each other again.

All married couples should have a date night at least once a week or more. Staying connected to your spouse and trying new things keeps the passion and love alive. Marriage is like a plant. You must keep it watered and be given enough sunlight so it can blossom. If not, it will wither away and die.

I was looking through Pinterest and found another great idea. The second part of his gift was even more creative. I bought a heart-shaped box that was filled with individual chocolate candies. Removing the candies out of the little plastic containers, and replacing them with coins, a hundred-dollar bill, two fifty-dollar bills, three twenties, two tens, and three fives and a couple of ones. This normal looking heart-shaped candy box was filled with money. Knowing that money is all that he seemed to care about, I knew that he would be pleased. Proud and anxious to give to him, I placed it in my drawer next to my bed.

The day before Valentine's Day, I received a call from Adam. He called to let me know that he would be coming home a day later.

"Why?" I asked. His answer was, "I need to get my oil changed and it's scheduled for tomorrow." Trying not to get mad but feeling like it was probably true but also an excuse to stay an extra day, I told him thank you for letting me know. We didn't talk long as I was at work.

While doing laundry at the salon, God spoke softly to me, "I am taking him away. He's not coming back the same. He's a new Adam." Then God added and showed me divorce papers and then him walking away and returning to me. Ignoring it as I had convinced myself he was back for good.

Waking up on Valentine's Day, I had an appointment with our accountant. After seeing our accountant and reviewing all the business finances, I called Adam to let him know about the taxes. He was so angry with me and blaming me for all the finances. I tried to explain to him of all the times he left us and took money and did all that he wanted to and not being there with me through the third salon that this was the consequences. He didn't want to hear the truth and ending our conversation, "Now how much do I owe? You can't do anything right." He hung up on me. All the memories and seeing all the money he had spent on her and his double life made me angry. I went back to the salon and printed out all the details of all three businesses and our bank statements. "I will show him exactly where everything went when he comes home," I thought angrily.

Coming back from the accountant, I received a text from Daxx's girlfriend showing me their new vehicle but more importantly noticing on her hand a beautiful engagement ring. Calling them both up and congratulating them asking when the big day was. They had mentioned the date November 11th. Choosing that date was easy for Daxx since it was Veteran's Day. He didn't want to ever forget his anniversary date. I was happy to see that Daxx had found the one for him.

Not even caring about the holiday as it was already ruined, I went to bed and waited for Adam to return the following day. Thinking twice about giving him his gifts.

The next day when I woke up, I headed into the dining room and sat at the table. I began spreading out all documents and bank statements. I was preparing everything to show him. I was done with him making me feel like I was a failure after all that I had been through with him. I had busted my butt in all our businesses for over eleven years and made some decisions without him as he had abandoned me time and time again.

When he arrived and walked into the house, his demeanor had changed dramatically. He seemed more distant and colder than when he left in January. Sitting him down and going through all the documents with a fine-tooth comb, I showed him exactly what it had cost us by him leaving our marriage now for over three years. I let him know that if anyone should be angry, it should be me as I am the one who hadn't received any paychecks for years. Everything I did I put back in the salon or I would invest in another salon thinking that was what he wanted.

"I don't deserve this, Adam. I did nothing wrong and I am tired of you blaming me for all of this. It's time you take responsibility for all that you caused." I cried out to him. Moments went by as he just stared at all the paperwork and then he looked at me and said, "We will take care of this." With some relief and seeing his mood had lighten up, I thought he had finally seen what I was trying to show him all along. I added, "This is how Satan took us down. He knew we didn't need the third salon. He destroyed us. Now that we have God in our lives and we both are on the same page, we can clean this mess up together." Adam just looked at me and grabbed my hand and nodded his head.

After putting a financial plan together, I gathered up the papers to put away and walked into our bedroom. I walked over to my drawer by my side of the bed and retrieved his gifts to give to him. He was walking in as I turned around. Handing both gifts to him in hopes that he would hand me something in return only to see his hand empty, I still smiled and asked him to open his gifts.

"More candy?" he said.

"Just open it," I replied. Watching him open the heart-shape candy box and seeing the lid had five scratch off tickets, he then noticed all the money sitting in front of him.

He smiled. "This is neat. Thank you."

I told him I used my own money and that it wasn't his money that he was looking at. He just chuckled and said, "Sure."

"Seriously, it's not, look at your account. You will see I didn't take anything out."

Then he opened the big three-foot card and could see all the little cards attached to it. He looked puzzled so I said, "Each time you come home, I thought we could have a date night and bring some fun back into our lives."

"Okay, that sounds good, thank you." Then he leaned over and kissed me.

"Since I didn't get you anything, we will take this money and go out to dinner, sound good?"

"Yeah, that's fine but you don't have to. It's yours." I was bummed to see that I didn't even get a card when I had noticed in our bank account that he had gone to a drug store and spent a little money. I had thought maybe he bought me a card.

Trying not to show disappointment, I suggested that we go over to see Ash and the boys seeing that he hadn't seen her new place yet.

Adam played with the boys for a while in their room. Eastyn was excited to show him all his toys and his bathroom and around the apartment.

My mom asked Adam what he thought of Ash's place in trying to make conversation. His reply was, "It's nice." Not convincing to my mother that he meant it. When my mom would try and talk to him, she felt he was cold and distant and sometimes judgmental on anything anyone would say.

Later that night, Adam and I were lying in bed while he was listening to documentaries of the dark web on his phone. Listening to all the negative footage and making me feel that evil was in our room, I asked him to turn it off. "Why? This is cool stuff. You should listen to this this could happen to you," he said.

"What do you mean?" I asked him.

"You need to be safe and make sure you are locking all the doors and leaving a light on at night. Where is the gun?" he answered back.

"Stop, Adam, you are scaring me. Where is all this negative attitude coming from? You are different. What is wrong with you?" I responded back with irritation in my voice.

Him not really responding, he shut it off and we went to bed. As I was laying there, I started questioning his behavior and wondering and asking what was really going on. I knew deep down something wasn't right and when I would ask him if he was still seeing Loren, he would get mad and tell me to quit asking him questions and that we we're fine, and everything was fine between us.

One afternoon while I was working and Adam was home hanging out waiting for me to get off, he would notice that when I would come home, I would either be in the kitchen or our bedroom. He had seen that our house was way bigger than we needed.

Adam and I always talked a lot in bed at night. "We could sell the house now. That would help pay down all our debt and credit cards," he suggested.

"Are you serious?" I asked surprisingly. He was even thinking about selling our home as this was his dream home that he wanted.

"We don't need this big house and noticed that when you come home, you are either in the kitchen or in our bedroom. You hardly even go downstairs," he acknowledged back.

Thinking about what Adam had suggested and asking God if this was what we needed to do, he then showed me a family in our home. A man and a woman with dark hair with two children. Then he showed me the middle part of July and put his hand down like a gavel, making it feel as if we would be out of here by the sixteenth.

With not saying anything else to each other, I drifted off to sleep.

REALTOR

Spring was around the corner, and Adam was back to work. We were getting into our prime season, which made it busier in the salons. My mother was staying with us and helping me in our businesses. I love spending time with her and knowing that God was keeping her close to us all for his reasons. We sometimes take "time" for granted and forget to cherish what we have with our loved ones while they are still here. After my father's passing, I began to look at life differently and wanted to share all I could with family and friends.

When she and I was working in our south location, she pointed out that we should put a fresh coat of paint on a few walls, making it brighter and more welcoming when clients would walk in. The wall behind the counter was a dark purple that made it look dark and dreary.

On a Sunday night after closing, we just did that. We painted three walls white. While my mother was taping and I was painting, suddenly, I saw the south location emerge down and then emerge back up like it was a new salon in my mind and God spoke, "New Sassy Tan and Spa."

Interesting after that, I started feeling as if I wasn't going to be working or even owning the salon much longer. "Am I supposed to sell this salon, God? What are you trying to show me?"

I felt like my life was about to change in more ways than one. I remember what God had spoken in November that he was reversing everything to make new. Asking him if he wanted me to sell our first location too, he immediately shouted, "No, this is where it all began. I am making it right again." I knew God was working hard in my life. Having to listen to him not knowing how everything was going to turn out, I waited for him to show me what to do next.

To keep my mind open about the changes that were starting to happen, I was happy to see that my book was moving along swiftly. The cover of the book was a struggle but a couple times of revising it, it looked perfect. Excited to hear from my publisher that my book should be ready in just a couple of months.

My phone began to ring and as I looked down from an unknown number, answering it hesitantly, "Hello?" "Hello, beautiful" was a voice that was cherry on the other end. Realizing it was my long-lost friend Amy, I was happy to hear her voice. "Hello, there, how are you?" I said in a happily voice.

Amy had moved to California in 2017. She was calling to let me know that she had moved back for good. After what had happened to our friendship that previous July of 2017, we continued to stay in contact through the months. Amy and I were working on our friendship and rebuilding trust. I was excited to hear that she had rekindled with an old love from her childhood and was living close by. We made plans for us to get together for our famous dinner that we both had missed sharing.

A couple of days later, Amy showed up while I was cooking taco meat and chatting with Ash in the kitchen. Crunching up Doritos and placing into a bowl and covering it with meat and cheddar cheese, our favorite meal was waiting for all of us. I know it doesn't sound too appetizing to others, but it was what we liked to eat. Washing it down with a Pepsi felt like old times and talking about the memories we had shared while all of us were going through hard times. We laughed and was excited to hear that she was getting married on Ash's birthday, September 23, 2018.

She played with the boys while Ash was catching her up on her life. We all shared bits and pieces of our lives with one another. She was so happy with her new fiancé and I was so excited to hear that he was a Christian man. She was learning so much from him, and she seemed calmer and was starting to hear God more. I shared with her all that was changing in my life and she was happy to see that Adam and I were still working on our marriage. We both were able to put our past behind us and focus on the future of our friendship.

With both of our dark days of playing with tarot cards and pendulums, it had been replaced with going to the same church and reading the Bible. It seemed as if Amy was on the right track and had let go of all the evil in her life and now was following God and doing what he had called her to do.

We had spent a couple more hours together until it was getting late. Her drive back to Denver was waiting for her and she knew she had work early the next morning. Ash and I walked her to the door, hugged one another, and waved to her goodbye.

When Adam returned on his days off, we met with a realtor. She came over to our home and did her evaluation of our property. There were a few things that needed to be fixed before selling. Our house was only four years old, so it was still practically brand-new. She felt that our house should sell quickly since the market was good and the location was in a prime spot.

After she left, Adam and I called different contractors to get the schedule work completed so it could be put for a listing. I asked him if this is what he wanted to do and if we were making the right choice. He said, "Yes." In asking him what or where would we go next, he answered with a vague, "I don't know. We will find somewhere else to live."

To break up some of his time, he and I took a day and drove all around the city looking at patio homes, townhomes, other homes, and decided that a patio home is what we wanted next. He didn't want the responsibility of maintenance any longer of a home and with our schedules so busy and him working away seemed the best solution. As we were driving, he was holding my hand and making me feel that we really were making a new beginning for the two of us. We talked about future things making it look as if our lives were on the same page.

Adam and I were waiting at the car wash for his vehicle to finish when Felecia called me. "Do you have a minute?" she asked.

"Yes, of course," she asked me to go into a room where Adam wasn't around, so I went into the bathroom. "I don't know how to say this, but God has been sharing this all day and I have to tell you," she said in a concerned tone.

"Just tell me, I need to know," I replied.

"Adam is preparing to leave," she voiced.

"Okay, that makes sense. I heard God in February telling me he was taking him again." Upset hearing that but knowing it was true I could feel that Adam was preparing to leave once our house sold. Felicia kept giving me the strength to continue trusting God, knowing he was doing his work and she said that she would be there for me through it all. Our conversation was short as Adam was waiting for me, but I knew what was about to come. I just didn't want to face it all over again.

Getting into the car and realizing the truth and knowing that God was preparing me in every way, I asked him, "Do you think we should sell the south location, so we only have one salon?"

He said, "If you want to."

Looking at him, I said, "If I want to, what about you? It's yours too?"

"See what you can do about selling it." Hearing his words with no emotional connection gave me the confirmation that he was planning on exiting out of my life for good.

Hearing once again, "He's not coming back the same" over and over in my head on the way back to the house puzzled me even more.

Getting back to the house, I began packing and putting dishes from our kitchen into boxes and storing in the garage. Not knowing how fast the house would sell and with me working a lot of hours, I only had so much time to get things done. Feeling like my life was going to be lonely I had to trust God. I knew he would show me what was coming next.

While packing, I began seeing a big bright kitchen that had a white table top. The place seemed to be very open and inviting. I shared my vision with Adam, but he just shrugged his shoulders and said, "Okay."

Later that night while Adam was playing on his phone and I was surfing on my computer, his mother called. She asked us if we wanted to go to Paris and Spain that following December. There was a Groupon advertising a great price. While she was still on the phone with me, I asked, "Your mother would like to know if we would like to join them in Paris and Spain in December?"

He responded, "Sure, I guess."

Feeling at that moment he really didn't want to, I told her I would call her back. After hanging up with his mom, I asked him again. His reply was, "It's far off to plan ahead now, don't you think?"

"Well, the price is good, but we only have two more days to purchase. It's up to you."

"Go ahead if you would like," was his final answer.

I should have listened to what God was trying to tell me but instead I was taking control of my life once again out of fear. Even as I tried purchasing the tickets, there were glitches. Our bank account was double charged instead of only once, which made me even more frustrated. Another sign that this trip wasn't supposed to happen, but I ignored it.

I called back Kitty to let her know that the tickets were purchased. We started preparing for the trip even though it was still months away.

After Adam had left to return to work, our house was being shown two to three times a week. With each showing the potential buyers would complain about how close we were to the main road and was concerned of the traffic noise.

In sharing with Adam over the phone, the frustration that our house wouldn't sell, he also seemed to feel what I was feeling. Once the decision was made to sell, I was ready to have a clean fresh start. The house that was built was no longer inviting to me. Every room had brought me so much pain of reliving all the lies, cheating, and deceit. I never even was able to experience joy with Adam in our swimming pool or one night alone under the moonlight. The house never really felt like a home as Adam was absent most of the time. It was more like a prison to me that held me captive for so many years. I prayed even and asked God to take away this house and to let me be free of all pain and memories.

My birthday was coming up and was happy to see that he would be home to celebrate with me. Arriving back home on my day, he handed me a card that had a one hundred fifty-dollar gift certificate to one of my favorite stores, "Go buy anything you want," he said to me as he watched me open the card.

"Thank you, I will. I need new clothes."

To end the day, my mother, Ash, Easytn, Brystyn, Adam and I all went out to dinner at a local steakhouse restaurant. The dinner was good but the feeling I was receiving from Adam was distant and cold.

My mother had bought me a little tablet so I could play games and do cross stitch. I thought the screen was big enough but found I wanted it a little bigger. While we were driving, I asked Adam if we could trade it in and asked if he could pay the difference. He seemed irritated that I had asked. "I guess," was his response. Making me feel like I was asking too much, I hesitated on trading it.

He drove to the store, and as we were walking in, he seemed to lighten up a little. Trading in my tablet for a bigger one, he also bought me a carrying case to go with it.

"Is that all you need now?" he asked.

"Yes, thank you, I appreciate it."

"You're welcome, now let's go back to the house," he said walking up to the cash out line to check out.

Later that night while we were lying in bed, he shared with me that he would be working extra days the next time he would be returning to work. We talked about if the house would sell while he was away that I would be the one who would have to move us.

Praying to God and asking if our house would sell soon, he began showing me a couple with dark hair and kids laughing. I could hear footsteps coming up from the downstairs. He began showing me that the middle of July we would be out of the house for good. Seeing the visions so close gave me relief that our house would be selling soon.

Out of the blue moments later, Adam made a comment about my book. He was concerned about all that I had written about him.

He was feeling like I made him out to be a bad person and that some things I had said weren't nice making him feel uneasy.

I had asked him over and over before submitting to the publisher if he wanted to read it. He had showed no interest in reading it, which brought up a red flag to me. "Why now does he care about all that I wrote after all this time? Everything I wrote was true." His comments made me question my book as it was about to be released to the world within a few weeks. I had started seeing my book arriving to our salon while Adam was standing next to me.

He left the next day for work. Each time he would leave, the feelings grew stronger that we were drifting apart.

My mother left shortly after Adam returned to work. Never liking to say goodbye to her, I knew I would be seeing her soon for a wedding in the summer. We both prayed that our house would be sold by then. She told me to stay strong and that she knew things were going to be okay regardless of my situation.

OH, BABY!

IT WAS NOW THE MONTH OF MAY. Our house had been on the market for a little over a month and still had no prospect buyers. I was beginning to think that we weren't going to sell and all the packing I did was for nothing. The visions I kept getting made me keep the faith as I knew God was in control of when the house would sell. Staying positive, I knew God had a better plan for me somewhere soon.

It is so hard in our lives to give up our control to God. We think that we know what is best for us. He is the one who created all of us on his own time and he knows exactly what he needs to do in order to bring things to our lives for our good. I have learned how to watch for God as he shows me how he moves chess pieces like in the game. He strategically decides how to move each one of the pieces to fit in our lives. We must have patience while he is at work.

Paul and Felicia were also selling their home as they were moving the end of the month into a home that was being built. There were struggles on and off with their home, but finally it was coming together and soon would be moving.

It seemed their realtor was fast at getting their house sold. I pondered to God and asked, "Should we get a new realtor too? Should we ask him to help us?" I didn't want to let go of our realtor, but I knew she had been stressed with her ill mother and every time Adam would call to see how the house was selling, I didn't have any good news to share with him. I felt once again I was failing him.

One night while Adam and I were on the phone we called our realtor and asked for her to release herself so we could go with Paul and Felicia's relator. She was very understanding, and she stepped away from selling our house with no hard feelings.

Adam was working extra days in the month, so a lot was put on my shoulders. The new realtor came and had one of his colleagues stage the house, so it looked more inviting to potential buyers. As I watched her do her magic in making each room come to life, I was feeling more optimistic that this was God's plan and that now our house would sell.

While all the changes that were happening, God still let me know that this was just the beginning and that after the house selling, my life would be even more intense. He kept telling me to trust him and to keep my eyes on him and that he was reversing everything to make new.

I kept busy in the salon as the days rolled by. One day while working, I started seeing my book closer in my mind and that Adam and Ash was standing next to me when it arrived in a box.

Adam was about to be off a few days later so I thought maybe it would arrive while he was home. I was so excited to see the finished project that I had been working on for so long.

Once Adam arrived home, I took a few days off to spend with him. While we were in the car, I shared with him the vision I had been seeing about my book and that he would be here to witness this exciting moment with me. "We will see is all he said."

I had said this before in previous chapters, of being tired and frustrated that he never believed me that God was speaking to me. I wanted to share so many things with him, but he never seemed interested. My clients seemed more interested in my life rather than my own husband. Each time he came home I felt him fading away from me and our life together.

Out of so much fear, I even would ask him if Loren was still in the picture, but he denied it to me time and time again. The bedroom spoke volumes to me as there had been no connection for several months now. I had stopped reaching for him and stopped asking any questions that involved us. I would lay in bed at night and go through all the visions that God had showed me over the years and asking myself if they were all true and if what I was seeing was real or asked if I crazy.

The next morning, Adam was driving me to work when Ash called excited, "Guess what came to the salon, Mom?"

"What, my book?" I asked with a smile on my face.

"Yep, it's here, come now so we can see you open it," she exclaimed.

Hanging up the phone, "See, I told you. I knew you would be here when my book arrived." I was looking over at him to see his response.

"Okay, we will go and check it out," he answered looking at me.

Walking into the salon and seeing the box from my publisher was surreal. Ash videotaped as I started opening the box. I was shaking and smiling with joy as I pulled out the master finish of my book. "I can't believe I did this. Is this real? Is this really my book?"

Staring back at me was my life story on how God saved me and how he had transformed my life. I was excited to share my story with others even though I knew it would make some people angry and not approve of my decisions. I was ready for all the controversy it would cause as I knew God had a bigger plan for my book and my life.

Thinking for a moment, about how too many times, people hide behind doors of their past, fear, anger, depression, sadness, failures in life, death, relationships, and abuse and not allow God in their lives so that he can mold and build character within each one of us. God has a hand in our lives to allow bad things to happen to us, but Satan instigates the process, which allows God to shape and mold us to become more like Christ in his image.

Think about this, if everything was going good in our lives, meaning we had the best job, all the money we ever wanted, the best marriage, best friends and families, the nicest house on the street, good health, etc., how would we ever have the need or the desire to come to our Savior for salvation? God wants us to chase him as much as he chases us to be in our lives. He wants to have a relationship with us just as we have relationships with our father, mother, sisters, brothers, friends, pets, and neighbors.

He knows the right way to get our attention when he is ready for the real work of our souls to begin. We are all broken in ways of our lives. His son died on the cross for us as he knew life didn't work the way we all thought or intended it to be. Christ knew their would-be trials and tribulations in each one of our lives.

"I am so proud of you." The words coming from the mouth of the only man who I ever wanted to please. "Thank you, babe, I needed to hear that." I smiled back at him. Thumbing through my book and seeing the words that I had written staring back at me just sent many chills throughout my body. "Thank you, God, you are the one who gave me the strength. Thank you." Looking up towards heaven with glory in hopes that I had made him proud.

One of our clients had walked in and was eager to purchase my very first copy. I gladly autographed it as I handed it to her. She and I had spoken many times about my book. We both attended the same church, so she understood how my life had transformed over the following year. I asked her for her honest feedback once she read it. I am the type of person who wants honesty. I wanted to hear how others view my book.

After all the excitement, Adam and I left the salon. I had asked him to buy shelves so that I could put in the salon to display my book. He said, "You don't need it right away. You still have to review the book and then order, it will take a few weeks." Not understanding why, he responded that way to my asking after hearing him say he was proud of me. I just looked out the window. In my mind, I was thinking, "That wasn't very nice. Thanks for ruining my moment."

He was leaving the next day, and to be honest, I was glad as I didn't feel like he even cared about anything anymore. His demeanor and attitude became cold and curt to me during our visit.

It was now getting toward the end of May. I had reviewed my book and gave the approval to my publisher to go ahead and to proceed with printing my book. The client who bought my book came in. "Where is the second book, I need to keep reading," she expressed.

I laughed and said, "I haven't written it yet, but God told me I would have three books."

"Well, it was really good. I couldn't put it down," she added.

"Well, that makes me feel good. Thank you for telling me."

"See, Heather, your book is making a difference already. You will see," is what I heard from God.

Our house was getting ready to be put on the market once again. Lying in bed each night, I would pray to God to please sell the house so we could start our lives over.

I noticed when talking to clients I would refer to "my" new place, instead of "our" new town home or apartment or place making me question why I was choosing different words. I would catch myself and ask myself is this a sign that I am going to be alone again?

One morning early around 4:00 a.m., I received a phone call from Adam. He seemed to be in a panic and rambling his sentences together, "My truck broke down and I left my wallet at the man camp. Before you check the bank account, I want you to know that I bought the guys pizza last night so you will see that I had spent more than usual." I thought, "Why is he telling me all this? What is he hiding now?"

Responding, "Where are you now? Are you at work? Where is the truck?"

Answering my questions, "I called a guy from work. He came to pick me up. The truck is on the side of the road, waiting to be towed." He added, "I think it might be the transmission."

"Okay, we will get it fixed, maybe you need to look at buying another truck," I suggested.

Bringing me back to a vision I had seen years ago of him buying a maroon truck flashed before my eyes quickly. We talked awhile longer and then hung up. As I was walking back into our bedroom, I started hearing Adam's voice again, "Please forgive me. It's the last time I will lie to you." What does this mean? What is going on? I hadn't heard Adam's voice in my head for a long time now. The feeling of despair and knowing there was more to his story haunted me as I tried going back to sleep.

When I awoke back up later in the morning, I looked at our bank account and saw the charges that he had spoken about. Appearing in front of me was Loren once again and seeing his wallet on a counter. Freezing in the moment trying to understand. "It's all happening again. He is leaving once the house sells. I just know it." Trying to face the ugly truth. She is still in the picture.

About a week later, my book had hit the Internet and was ready for the world to see. I had shared with Adam the good news that it was out for purchase and I was looking forward to hearing people's reviews.

Not even a couple of days later, Adam called me in the morning and asked if I knew this guy who had just posted a review of my book. Supposedly he was from Denver. Adam shared with me that it was a horrible review and the guy even made bad comments like I wasn't hearing God and that my husband was still living with his girlfriend and that I was a fake and a phony.

I was so angry when Adam read that to me. At that moment, I asked him if he was still living with Loren and if all of this was true? He denied it all and said it was probably just some random guy. I didn't believe any of it and all the behavior Adam was portraying was making sense to me that he still was seeing her and that he never left her.

I had detached myself from Adam from that moment on as much as I could. I knew God was preparing me through his strength. I could feel his strength and I knew he would show me the way and wouldn't leave me.

Feeling like my book was a mistake and wished I had never put it out there, Satan was getting a good laugh at me. Satan finds every little crack and cranny to steal your joy away.

Trying to keep a brave face on and still holding on to hope that after the house would sell that Adam would stay, is all I prayed about even though I knew what was ahead for me.

It was the week of memorial weekend when more stunning news came. "*Mom!*" was a loud scream coming from the bathroom off the kitchen. I was in our bathroom cleaning when Ash came rushing in to show me a positive pregnancy test.

My mouth dropped open and said, "Really? I thought you were taking the pill and being careful?"

With tears in her eyes as she fell onto her knees, looking up at me, she said, "I was, not this again. I don't want to be pregnant."

Kneeling and holding her, I told her that we would get through this and that God had a plan.

Immediately God reminded me of the vision I had seen the previous November that someone would be pregnant by Daxx's wedding. Seeing the visions coming true gave me clarity that I wasn't crazy and that God was working in my life whether I understood it or not.

As I shared the news with Adam, he seemed to be concerned of Ash's state of mind. I gave the phone over to her so he could talk to her. He gave her the reassurance that he would be there for her and that it would be okay. Hearing that gave me hope for us too. That day we let the news sink in that Ash was having her third child.

The next day as I was working, Adam called me and asked, "Have you been on Facebook?"

"No, why?"

"You know your friend Amy, she died yesterday."

"What? Are you serious?" I reached for my phone in shock to look onto her Facebook page to see that it was true. "This can't be true. I just seen her a few months ago," I told Adam.

I thanked him for telling me but had to go as I was in tears. Calling Ash immediately to let her know the sad news and when she asked when she passed, I told her the day before, she reminded me that was the same day, she found out she was expecting. Once again proving that God's timing is perfect in every way. While God took and angel from us, he brought us a gift. A new life. Ash started crying and came over to the salon.

After the shock wore off, I began remembering conversations that we had had exactly two years ago while she was with Ash and me in our house one evening. Bringing me back to May 2016. When I would see Amy, I would feel my chest hurt and I could feel "death" around her. Having and sharing so many conversations about it as the feelings were so strong and we could talk about anything, Amy shared that when she would try to think about her future or try to see herself years down the road everything looked and felt empty and black. She could never see herself living long which made Ash and I confused and sad.

Amy had gone through a lot in her life and had so much pain that she felt she wasn't supposed to live long. Trying to change the subject and not think negatively, we started talking about other things like her grandchildren. Her grandchildren gave her life and gave her so much happiness.

Around the time I started seeing this, she had been dating an older gentleman, so I thought maybe I was seeing his death. Thinking maybe he was going to have a heart attack since their age difference was over fifteen years. Amy was just forty-four. I sure didn't think it would be her.

Looking back on that night and that intense conversation that felt so uncomfortable, I now know God was showing me her death. Amy and I had so many good conversations about God. I knew she was in heaven with him making me feel closer to her. I now had one of my best friends and my father watching over us along with God.

The next day I reached out onto Facebook to her fiancé and asked him to call me. I had never spoke or met him and hoped that he would answer back. A few moments later, my phone rang, and it was him. He shared with me that she died of a heart attack. It was fast and sudden. She had been getting pain in her chest earlier in the morning and finally decided to go to the hospital after the pain wouldn't go away. Her fiancé put her into his truck in the passenger seat and went back in to retrieve her purse from the house. When he climbed into the driver's side and looked over to her, she was already gone. He tried saving her, but it was too late.

I shared with him the vision that I had a couple of years earlier. He believed in visions as he was deep in the Faith and with God. He began to share with me her struggles he had been seeing in her life. He tried so hard to get her to see that God was with her and that she needed to change her outlook on life. He loved her so much and knew that she was his soulmate.

We both cried over the loss of Amy and he let me know how much she would talk about me and Ash. She was always ashamed of what she had put me through that July of 2016. I assured him that we made amends and our friendship was strong again.

It is so important to forgive the ones who have hurt us in our lives. We may never get the chance to and for some it may be too late and then you are left with the regrets and anger within yourself. So, if someone has ever done you wrong, please find it in your heart to forgive and let God be the one to take care of your pain and the person who harmed you. It isn't your place to judge and act out your own pain to harm others.

The day of her funeral while Ash was driving, I opened my book to see where I had put her in my storyline. Noticing that on page 143 was where her name began, most of us knows that it means "I LOVE YOU." Looking at each other we immediately smiled with tears knowing that was a sign from Amy as she always said, "I love you, girls."

Once we arrived to the church, Ash and I were standing over her casket in disbelief. It didn't even look like the spunky, loving Amy that we once knew. She looked like an old woman wearing a dress color that she would have never chosen for herself. We couldn't even look at her. We wanted to remember her the way we knew her. I could see her happy, smiling and wearing a red blouse and a pair of shorts. Red was her favorite color.

I walked into where her mother was and gave her my book and explained to her that she was a big part of my life and that I had written a book on faith and wanted her to have a copy of it as her daughter was in my book. I even shared a copy with her sister in hopes they could see what an impact their daughter, her sister had on our lives.

During the funeral, I had no intentions of getting up and speaking but when they showed a video of her life and saw that Ash and myself were included, it made me realize how much we really meant to her and I needed to talk among her family and friends.

Ash walked up with me as we approached the podium. Looking out into the rows and seeing her adult children and grandchildren who were under the ages of nine, dressed in black suits staring back at us, I could see and feel their loss and suffering. With the strength from God and now with Amy, I began to speak to each one of them letting them know how much she had loved them whether they knew it or not. I wanted them all to know that they meant the world to her.

With tears rolling down my face, I kept it together enough to make each one laugh and to remind her loved ones of the joy that she had given us all. All agreeing that now she was our angel looking down upon us.

Leaving the funeral, we all gathered at her gravesite and said one last goodbye.

Selling of the House

With the warm sun shining as summer was beginning, we were getting more showings of our house. We were able to open the pool, turn on the waterfalls so when potential buyers would come, they would be able to envision themselves and could see what it would be like living in this beautiful place.

Our relator was keeping close tabs on us and felt that we would be getting offers soon. I kept on looking forward and was ready to sell and move out. With each passing day visions of the house selling and us moving was coming closer and closer to my mind.

While working one morning in the salon, one of my previous managers, CC, came into tan. She was preparing for her wedding and needed to tan for her special day.

This one day as she was walking in, I noticed a puzzle look on her face. Before I could ask her what she was thinking, she said, "I had a weird dream last night."

"What was it about?" I asked.

"I dreamt I quit my job at the bank and came to work for you full-time."

Looking at her, I laughed and just blurting the words came out, "Well, just buy the south salon, you have always wanted to own your own business."

She just looked at me and you could see for the both of us that something had changed instantly. "I will talk to my fiancé and get back with you," she said to me after her tanning session was over. She finished cleaning her bed and added that she wouldn't take it over until after her wedding. Her wedding was just a month away. I completely understood she needed to get through the most stressful time in planning her wedding before taking on something even bigger.

That evening in talking to Adam, I expressed the interest of CC wanting to purchase the south salon. He seemed pleased to hear and approved of it.

Going to sleep that night with some relief that things were moving in our direction, I asked God if this is the person who was supposed to buy our salon. Immediately he said yes and showed her working in that location. He also showed me again a couple with kids buying our house and he strongly and sternly said July sixteenth. He showed me that I would no longer be in this house.

Waking up to feeling the anticipation and the heaviness that things were about to change, I kept reminding myself that God was in control and I needed to trust him even when I was so unsure of my future. I read scriptures, continued journaling and listened to Christian music. I had noticed when I would journal, I would hear the same mantra of things I had heard over the years, but when I tried to think about the future, it looked completely different. I was getting the sense that timing on Gods part is everything and that I needed to be patient.

While Adam was home on his days off, we continued cleaning up around the yard, the backyard and the shed. He began selling things that we didn't need or use. With him selling things made me very uncomfortable. Like he was getting rid of things to make it easier for him to leave. I tried having conversations about our future and when asked where we would go next, he said, "I don't know we will find something. We don't need anything expensive just something to get us by until we finish taking care of business." His responses made me feel like the carpet of my life was going to be pulled out from under me.

One morning after breakfast, we were sitting in the living room in separate chairs. It was just him and me. Not knowing what to say, he grabbed my hand and asked, "Do you think I killed it all?"

Looking at him, I asked, "What do you mean?"

Again, he asked, "Do you think I killed us and the feelings I have for you? Did I do too much damage to our marriage?"

Tears began welting up inside of me as I looked at him and said, "Maybe. I know you still can't have intimacy with me. I don't know if it is out of guilt or shame. I know I don't deserve this." I asked him, "Do you want to go our separate ways?"

He replied back, "Some days yes and some days no, I am not willing to let you go. I know you deserve better and I know I have destroyed us. I don't know." He squeezed my hand and said we will get through this and gave me the smile like he really meant it.

Looking at him with a look of hope, I said, "Maybe once we sell the house and we get something with just the two of us we could start our life over. I don't want our marriage to end." He just looked at me not saying a word, but he climbed out of the chair and grabbed my hand to pull me out of the chair to embrace me. "We will work on this together he said as he was hugging me." With a feeling of relief, I squeezed him even harder.

I couldn't help but think of our conversation all day. I knew something was changing and I could feel the struggle that was going on inside of Adam and myself.

His two weeks went by fast, and before I knew it, it was Sunday Father's Day. We drove his corvette to church and noticed a car show in the parking lot of the church. It sparked an interest in Adam, so after the service, we started walking around looking at all different kinds of cars from the 1920s to today's collections.

He seemed to be enjoying looking at the beautiful cars when a guy from church made a comment about Father's Day and was happy to see Adam was out with his wife. He made me and the other guy uncomfortable with the comment he made about trading in what you already have and try out other models just for fun. Making me feel like he was trading me in for a newer model. When the guy looked at me, I could tell by his face that it was a warning for me to be prepared. Interesting how God uses other individuals to give us messages that he is trying to tell us. That comment and the unsettlement I was feeling stayed with me the rest of the day.

Once we were done looking at the cars, we met Ash and the boys for lunch. Ash noticed Adam seemed more irritated and annoyed. Eastyn was acting up and throwing a fit which intensified his mood even more. Ash and I tried to make small conversation to lighten up the mood. I was telling her on the way over that we have another showing coming in that week and I was praying that the house would sell soon.

Knowing that another showing was happening in a few days, I wanted to get the house ready even more. Ash and all of us went back to the house so the kids could swim, and I could start to clean. Once we got back to the house, I went downstairs and started vacuuming the entire basement.

Ash had noticed that Adam was on his phone talking to Loren on some social media site. It had only been two minutes from their last communication. She immediately told me, and I confronted him asking him if he was still talking to her and shared what Ash had just seen. He denied it and said that it must have still been on there from months previously. Does he really think I am that stupid? Looking at him and knowing that he couldn't lie to me anymore, I left the room and went back downstairs to continue cleaning.

Meanwhile Adam was upstairs packing his suitcase as he and Daxx were getting ready to leave for work.

"That's how you vacuum?" he questioned as he came walking down the stairs.

"What do you mean?" I asked looking at him puzzled.

"Where are the lines to show that you have vacuumed, looks like you are doing it half ass."

I thought he was joking as I had just started and wasn't even finished. I had moved the vacuum head down lower so that when vacuuming you would be able to see the lines. I was appalled with what he was saying. He turned into this angry mean person who was saying hurtful words to me. After realizing he wasn't joking, I defended myself and started yelling back at him.

Ash must have heard us arguing as she came downstairs, and Adam couldn't help himself to belittle me even more. "Ashley show your mom how to vacuum the proper way."

At this point, I was in tears and couldn't understand how he could be so cruel. As he walked up the stairs, he said, "I'm out of here and went into our bedroom and grabbed his suitcase and headed for the door."

Shocked to see this was how our time was going to end, I asked, "You are leaving for four weeks like this, no kiss, no hug, no nothing?"

"Yep, see you later!" and got into his truck where Daxx was sitting and waiting for him.

I knew I couldn't go and chase him, so I just slammed the door and went back into the house. Ash was waiting for me and asked, "What just happened?"

"I don't know, I don't understand. He just turned into this mean person suddenly and created this fight before he left. It had nothing to do with the vacuum." I began crying. Ash hugged me and told me that he was lying and that he was just talking to her. Knowing Ash was right and not wanting to believe it, the truth was staring right at me.

After what happened, I had made a promise to myself that I wasn't going to call or reach for him while he was away. I was reminded about our conversation we had a few days earlier and felt he needed this time to figure out what he wanted.

I couldn't help but think about earlier that afternoon at church and how he had been acting. It started making sense to me that the comment he was making was something he really felt and was wanting to do but didn't have the courage to be honest with me.

In talking with Felicia, she helped me to stay positive and focus on our bright future. She assured me that things would be okay even if he was to leave that he would be back and that God had a bigger plan for us both.

A couple of days had gone by with no contact with Adam. While sitting in the doctor's office a text came through from him apologizing to me for the way he treated me and told me that he was working on himself and that he would see me soon. Not sure if I should respond, I waited for a while before replying to him.

I will admit I was very frustrated with God and couldn't understand what he was doing to me and why this was happening all over again. The agony and pain I was feeling was so dark and dreary.

On my knees I asked for clarity on what I needed to do with my life. In a stern voice from God, he spoke very clear, "Keep your eyes on me. I am bringing Adam back a different man." I thought, "How many times have I heard this before?" It's okay to admit when we get angry with God. He is our Heavenly Father and although we have "earthly" fathers, we all agree that we get angry with them from time to time. It is God's right to do whatever he needs to do to us in order to get us to listen to him.

Looking up a verse to help me understand what he was trying to say to me, I went to Romans 8:28: "And we know that God causes everything to work together for the good of those who love God and are called according to his purpose for them."

Rereading that verse repeatedly, I was trying to understand what God was trying to show me. It was him who led me to that verse at that moment. I don't think we realize or recognize when God is trying to speak to us. He knows exactly at the precise time and the right circumstance we need in our lives to grow us. It's our job to watch and look for him to guide us each day with having trust and faith in only him. We cannot control our own lives. We may think we can, but the path we choose may be long and winding and painful and we later find if we had just listened to him for his direction our path could have been straighter.

Knowing that God was in control of my life, I could feel his arms around me and could feel his love. Reminding me of times when my father would hug me to make me feel safe and secure.

He showed me once again that our house would be selling, and we would be out of the situation in the middle of July.

The day of the showing had arrived. Anticipation was building up inside of me and I kept praying that this is the one. Letting Adam know that the showing was happening he was hoping to that it would finally sell.

Waiting for our relator to call after the showing felt like eternity. It was like waiting and watching for a pot of water to boil.

Still working at the salon, I heard my phone ring while I was cleaning a tanning bed. Hurriedly I walked up to the front to answer it. Seeing it was our relator, I was hoping for good news. "They want to make an offer," he said to me right away.

"Seriously?"

"Yes." Getting all the details, I then called Adam and we had a three-way conversation. After us both listening to our relator, Adam asked if we could call him back in five minutes after discussing it with me.

The offer was a little lower than what we were asking but it was still a good offer that would get us to a good place. "I think we should take it," was his response to me. "I will do whatever you want, Adam. I am on your side and I am ready to start my life over with you." Waiting for him to agree with me and reassure me that we would start over, silence was on the other end instead. Moments went by and then, I said, "I will call our relator back and let him know we will take it." Hanging up the phone excited one way but disturbed in another I let the realtor know that we accepted their offer. "Great, I will let them know," he said. "I will call you with a closing date."

Calling back the next day, he said that our closing date would be July twenty-third. Hearing that I just smiled. God had showed me that we would be out of the house by July sixteenth. Another confirmation that God was showing me his timing is always perfect. It was June twenty-ninth, so I knew I had only a few weeks to get everything done. Adam was scheduled to fly in on July seventeenth so having a lot to do I started calling to get a moving truck to arrange with our schedule.

I was sitting in my favorite chair on our patio looking at the mountains. It was finally sinking in that the house was sold and now a new journey was about to begin. I began praising God and thanking him for all that he was doing for me and asked him where I should look for our new place. Waiting in silence, he whispered, "Champions at Norwood." He reminded me when Ash and I was driving a few months back I had written that place down and Pine Bluffs. Ash was about to move from her old apartment into Pine Bluffs in less than a month. So Ash and I drove over to Champions like God instructed me to do.

Walking in, we were greeted by the friendly staff. The lady showed us two different apartments, and when I saw the first one, I knew this was where we were supposed to be.

Months earlier once we had decided that we would sell our home, God had showed me that the kitchen we would be living in was open spaced and light color like white or gray. So, when I saw the kitchen, immediately it was confirmed to me this was where we would be. God kept saying to me, "This is the one."

After taking a tour of the gym, the outside pool, game room, and the barbeque area, the feeling grew even stronger and I was beginning to see us living here. There was a moment before calling Adam for his approval that I felt I would be the only one living here which my gut gave me the jab that let me know something big was about to change.

Even though I couldn't ignore it I called Adam happy, asking him if we could get it. His first question was, "Is there an extra garage for my corvette?"

"Yes, and there is a garage attached to our apartment. I have us on the first floor." I began sending him pictures to show him what it looked like. In calling him to see what he thought of the pictures, he said, "If you like it, I like it."

"Well, that doesn't sound very good," was my response to him.

"We'll get if you like it." Hearing a voice of no care from him, I knew that this was going to be my apartment and that he was leaving. It was clear to me even though he didn't come right out and say it.

Adam helped me with the paperwork through emails and secured the place for ten months. He didn't want a year lease, so we settled with ten. Knowing what I was feeling and what was about to come, I started planning for a future alone.

The week before we had to move out, a lot of things were happening in the house to confirm with me that God was preparing me for my new beginning.

One afternoon while I was packing, I had noticed that one of the grandchildren dropped a play spoon in between the screen of the fireplace. I asked Ash to help me get it out but there was no way we could reach it and drag it out from behind the screen. There was an extra covering part to the fireplace that made it impossible to retrieve the spoon. "I guess it will just have to stay in there. I can't get it," I said looking at Ashley.

"Yeah, Mom, there is no way we can get it," she said back to me.

She and I left for the day. She went back to her place and I went back to the salon to finish closing for the day.

As I walked out of the door into the garage, I looked up over six feet above my head and noticed the thick, hardwood covering to the attic was slightly opened. "How am I going to close that? I don't have a ladder tall enough to get to it." Getting into my car, I called the realtor and asked him if he had a ladder and if he could bring it over to fix it. I had a ladder at the salon, but I had no way of getting it into my car. He said he would be over later to fix it. Being thankful that our relator was so helpful and willing to do whatever he could to make this transition at ease was a blessing from God. He too was very strong in his faith, so I knew I was in good hands no matter what.

Later, that night after closing, I drove home. As I was pulling into the garage, I noticed that the attic door was shut once again. "Thank you," I said after seeing it was fixed. I didn't want to text our realtor as it was late but knowing he was coming over the next day to help me with some other things I knew I could thank him then.

The next morning our realtor showed up. I opened the door to him and said, "Thank you for fixing the attic door."

He looked at me stunned and said, "I am here now to fix it."

Looking at him, I said, "What, it's fixed. I thought you came over last night while I was gone."

At this time, we both started walking toward the door to the garage so I could show him that it was fixed. The day before I had sent him a picture from my phone showing him how the door had slid so he knew that it needed to be fixed. We both just looked at each other and questioned how this got fixed without either one of us.

I walked him over to the fireplace to show him that the spoon was wedged in between the fireplace and the covering and asked him he could get it out. He tried but was not able to reach the spoon. He said that it would be fine. I laughed and said, "It has to be fine."

We were both still trying to figure out what was going on in the house and scratching our heads asking how could this be. He even took the ladder out and climbed up to make sure that the attic door was closed properly. "It looks good and secure," he said to me, trying to move it but couldn't.

"Okay, great, thank you for checking it," I said back to him as he was climbing down.

Finishing up a few more things he then left, and I began more packing. Packing up a four-thousand-square-foot home wasn't easy. I was thankful that I had started earlier in the months and had placed boxes in the spare rooms.

It was late in the evening and after moving boxes, I was exhausted, so I went to bed. My conversations with Adam were short and brief. I had even tried telling him the weird things that was happening in the house, but I could tell he wasn't very interested.

It was just a few days away before Adam was to return home. Ash and the boys had come over to visit with me. With Ashley being a little over two months pregnant, I didn't want her to move any boxes so she helped me pack what she could. She walked over to the mantle above the fireplace and picked up the spoon and said, "Oh, you got it out?" Not sure what she was referring to I looked up from packing a box and she was holding the spoon in front of her face. Jumping in disbelief I asked, "How did you get it out?"

"I didn't, Mom, it was sitting on top of the mantle."

"You got to be kidding me?" I exclaimed back. I walked over to the mantle and investigated the fireplace and the spoon was no longer there. I held the spoon and sat down on the ledge of the fireplace in total shock. After a few minutes, I said to Ash, "Something is going on but what? What is God trying to say to me?" Ash didn't know what to say. I had told her about the attic incident, and she knew something was going on but couldn't help me. In the midst of it all, I was relieved to see the spoon situation had been resolved.

The night before Adam was due in from the airport, I was in my room relaxing in my chair. With a pen in one hand journaling and holding my bible in the other, I prayed for God to show me anything to help me. The pit in my stomach was so intense of fear that anyone could have cut a knife through the darkness of it. The only thing I kept hearing was, "Adam is not coming back the same. I have got this, keep your eyes on me." Holding on to those words of encouragement was what I needed.

Suddenly I heard the television on downstairs. I perked up in suspense and headed for the downstairs to look at what I was hearing. Since I was the only one living in the house, I knew I couldn't have been the one turning on the television. Walking down the stairs, slowly God reminded me of another time when our television turned on in our room. It was in the middle of the night and I had turned to Adam scared. It wasn't too shortly after that that Adam left once again.

Coming back to reality there it was. God was getting my attention to let me know that Adam was leaving again and that God had been preparing me for this turn of event.

12

REDECORATING

DRIVING TO THE AIRPORT, I WAS NERVOUS to see Adam. It had been over four weeks since we had seen one another. We had left on bad terms, but I was trying to be optimistic about our situation the best way I could. I had spoken to him briefly before he boarded his flight.

As I pulled into the arrival area, I could see him from a distance. Noticing his face didn't seem too happy to see my car pulling up my stomach began to turn into knots. "Here we go, I just know it," I said out loud to myself. He opened the back door and placed his back pack in the backseat. Not seeing a suitcase confirmed to me even more that he wasn't staying. He climbed in on the passenger side which was unusual for him. Any other time I would pick him up, he would take over and drive us home after he would reach for me to give me a hug and a kiss. He was very cold and distant to me when he looked at me. Feeling that energy from him I knew not to say too much and not to reach for his hand. The drive over to the house was very quiet and cold. I didn't even know what to say. I kept waiting for him to just blurt it out to me, but he kept quiet.

When we got home, he walked into the empty house. You could hear it echo as nothing was really left. I had given so much stuff away as I wanted us to start over completely with new furniture and new things to try and rebuild us. Still hoping that there was a new beginning for us together despite how things looked to me.

We walked into our old bedroom, so we could begin taking apart our bed frame so it would be easier for the movers to move. He seemed short with me when asking for different tools making me feel like I was more of a problem than anything else. He put the mattress on the floor. It was getting late so we both laid on the mattress. I tried making small talk with him, but he turned away from me talking to me and told me to get some sleep as we have a busy day coming up.

Waking up the next morning, I had to go and get the keys for our new place while Adam stayed back waiting for the movers to come. Upon returning with the keys and seeing the big moving truck with all our things, we were ready to leave. I was happy to leave behind all the bad memories that had happened in our once beautiful home. Looking forward to a new chapter in our lives. I was excited to show Adam our new place still hoping that what I was feeling wouldn't be coming true.

Arriving to our new place and opening the door, he walked around to each bedroom and bathroom. "Do you like?" I asked as he came walking from the hallway.

"Yeah, it's nice," he replied.

After the movers left, we started putting our bed frame together. The feeling in the room was heavy and the feelings grew more intense that he wasn't staying. I tried making conversations with him and tried getting him to joke around but it was like he wasn't even here.

I went out into the kitchen to unpack more boxes. The movers had put most of our boxes in the garage, so I moved them into the living room. A few hours went by and to break up the monotony we left for lunch.

While we were driving, I said, "We need to get furniture. Can we go to American Family Furniture?"

"Yes, after lunch, we will go see what we can find." We stopped off at a fast-food place, ate quickly, and then left.

Walking around the furniture store looking for a living room set and end tables and chairs, God was whispering to me, "It's going to be okay. Don't doubt me. He's not coming back the same." God was with me right along my side giving me comfort. I tried getting his opinions on what to buy. "Pick out what you want. Whatever you choose is fine with me." With his response, I picked out what I wanted. I stopped asking him anything and showed the salesman everything I had chosen. After paying, the salesman told me that the delivery would be that Friday which was two days away.

After leaving the furniture store, we went to Walmart to pick out more things for our apartment. Looking for bathroom accessories and items to match, Adam told me to hurry up and to pick anything as he wanted to leave. I was now getting madder at the way he was talking to me and I started to snap back to my defense.

It was late when we got home. I was emotionally tired and physically exhausted from all the moving. While lying in bed I could feel the distance from him even more when trying to hug him. I rolled over turning away from him and fell asleep.

The next morning, I got up early and went into the garage to bring in more boxes to finish unpacking. I had asked Adam to call the cable guy to get us set up for cable. Walking into our bedroom, I heard Adam on the phone setting up the service when he asked me, "Can you afford $103.00 a month?" Looking at him in question, "me or us?" He didn't wait for my answer and told the guy yes and to set us up. I walked out of the room and out into the garage.

A few moments later, Adam came out into the garage and started helping me rearrange and he organized is tool box area. He cleaned up shelves and moved storage tubs. At one point, he showed me how I would have to open the garage by hand if the remote wouldn't work. While he was showing me, I was wanting him just to tell me that he was leaving. I couldn't take it anymore.

I had broken down boxes and placed them in the back of our car. I looked over at him and said, "Let's take these to the dumpster."

"Okay."

We both got into the car. We were close to the salon when I felt his hand reach for mine. I had been looking out the window when I turned to him. Tears were falling down his face. He squeezed my hand even harder when I asked him, "What is wrong, Adam?"

At this point, he was really crying when the words that I knew were coming for a while now finally was said, "I can't stay." He cried out.

"I know. I have known you weren't staying. I have felt it for a while now. God prepared me," I said back with tears now falling from my face. "Why can't you stay?"

"I love you, but I don't have those feelings for you that a husband should have for a wife," was his answer to me. "I prayed to God for the answer. I have been struggling with this. I have to let you go."

I grabbed his face and looked him in his eyes and asked, "Are you still seeing Loren?"

"No, there is no one. I need to be on my own."

"Are you sure? Can't we try?"

"I have tried. I am no good for you. You deserve better."

"You are right. I do deserve better, thank you. The devil really has you now."

After talking longer and taking the boxes out of the back and throwing into the dumpster, we headed back to my apartment.

I walked into my bedroom and sat on my bed and cried even more. He came in and sat down with me and grabbed me to hold me. He kept telling me he was sorry, but this was for the best and that he was saving me. I wiped my tears and reached for a piece of paper to start writing down all the finances. With the closing of the house and the money that we would be getting, we decided on what was all going to be paid. He agreed to pay me a certain amount of money each month.

"Do you want to go and file now for divorce?" I asked him.

"If you want to, let's go now," was his response, thinking about it and almost saying yes, he retracted and said, "No, let's wait and get through the rest of the year for tax purposes. We will file next year."

"Okay," I said. "What about the wedding and our trip to Paris? The Paris trip is already paid for."

"I am not going. You can go if you want to and you can also go to the wedding if you want to. It's your family too."

"No, I will not be going if we are not together. It would be too hard on me," I said back.

Looking at my finger and seeing my wedding ring was still on my hand, I slipped it off and laid it on the bed. Adam then took his ring off and placed it by mine. I then picked them both up and placed in my jewelry box.

We were still talking when Ash came walking in. She could see that I was crying. "What's wrong?" she asked me.

"He's leaving again." I began crying even harder. She came over to me and hugged me. Adam started crying again and hugged her and told her what he had told me. Ash asked him the same question that I did.

"Are you still with Loren?"

Adam answered back, "No, I am not. I have no reason to lie if I was now. I love your mom but not the way a husband should love her."

Ash looked at me and said, "Mom, it will be okay. You don't want a man who can't love you the way you deserve. Adam is doing the right thing by telling you and being honest."

"I know but it still hurts. After all, we have been through, this is how it is going to end. It's hard for me to picture my life without him." Ash grabbed me and just held me letting me cry in her arms.

Adam had walked out of the bedroom and was standing in the kitchen when Ash and I came out of the bedroom. He was still crying, and we all embraced one another. He told her that no matter what he would be there for her and the boys. She had asked him he was going to move to Texas, and he said he didn't know what he would be doing but mostly likely he would since his job was there. He had told us both that he would be staying in the man camp until he could find a place. He made us both believe he was really going to be on his own for the first time without any other women.

Adam wanted to barbeque steaks and asked Ash to stay to eat with us. While Adam and I were sitting on our patio while he was cooking, I asked him if this was really the end of us?

"I don't know." He looked over at me. Hearing those words gave me hope. Hearing God at that moment say to me, "It's not over. He's not coming back the same."

A feeling of peace came over me. "If you do come back, we would need to start over. I would travel with you and not be apart from you. This is what killed our marriage. We have spent over nine years apart. We don't even know each other anymore."

"You are right. We would have to do things differently."

The steaks were done. Everyone ate but me. I had no appetite. My life was now a big empty hole again. You would think I would be used to this by now watching him come and go over the years but the pain of losing my husband all over again after a year of his return was still the same.

Ash and the boys left awhile later. The devastation was sinking in that this would be the last time Adam would be in my life. I finished up his laundry and unpacked a few boxes that were left. I stayed silent as I had nothing more to say. The words that Adam told me finally made me realize that he didn't love me anymore like a husband should love his wife. I trusted that he was telling me the truth that he needed to be on his own and he needed to find himself again.

It was getting late and I knew that we had to be up early so I could take him to the airport. I decided to sleep in our spare room. What good would it do for me to sleep in a bed with a husband who didn't feel the same? As I climbed into bed Adam hollered, "Aren't you coming to bed?"

"I am in bed," I responded back.

"Please come in here," he asked one more time.

Laying there for a moment, I asked God, "What should I do?"

Hearing a soft whisper voice coming from him, "Trust me, he's not coming back the same. Back in a flash." Immediately the vision came to me that he was knocking on the outside of my front door, and when opening it, I didn't know if I wanted to see him or if I even wanted him. The vision felt as if it was a long time before we had seen each other. It felt like the same vision I had seen in 2015. "That's weird. Why am I still seeing and feeling this again?"

Walking into the bedroom where Adam was laying, he said, "Come here. I want to hold you." Not understanding why, he would want me next to him since he was leaving but knowing it was the last night we would lay as a married couple, I climbed into bed with him. He wrapped his arms tightly around me and kept telling me he was sorry and that he never meant to hurt me. It was something within him that he still needed to find, and he knew it wasn't fair to keep me hanging on. Always feeling safe in his arms no matter what the circumstances were in our lives, it felt good to have him hold me.

We began talking about our past seventeen years that we had shared together. I admitted to him where things went wrong for me. I had told him I had wished that we had God in our lives from the beginning.

I could feel he was confused and conflicted with his decision and asked for me not to tell Big Ashley or Daxx or any of the family until he knew for sure on where this was going.

We were still on social media together as a couple, and he said that he wasn't going to change any status. With him saying that gave me comfort and hope that maybe things might change. I had told him that I wouldn't date anyone until the divorce was final. I knew that no matter what he was going to do I couldn't live in the sin if I was to date. Christ was now indwelling within me all the time and I knew what he expected of me.

Even in moments of our conversations we still found areas of laughter and joy that we talked about. We both shed tears and held each other. We had always had a good friendship from the very beginning so I was at least hoping that we could stay friends. Adam had impacted my life in so many ways that despite of all the pain he had put me through, I still found him to be a human being who was still a good person deep inside. I could see that he was still struggling letting me go.

"I know I am supposed to be with you, but I just can't give you what you want and need," he sadly said to me.

"I know. I am sorry that you stopped investing in us. I understand you lost the feelings for me. I know I have done everything to save my marriage. This is all on you."

I had nothing more to say so I rolled over and went to sleep. My eyes were hurting and heavy from all the crying. My body felt like an empty shell and my heart was shattered into pieces again. I prayed to God to please help me through this and to give me the strength to move on.

The next morning came too fast. Lying in bed and dreading to face that this was the end of us, I somehow by the grace of God got out of bed. Adam had been up and was getting ready to take a shower.

While he was in the shower, I was making the bed. While putting on the quilt a flash of my calendars that I had made and some of my journal entries came to my mind. After tidying up the bed, I walked over to the dresser and pulled out the calendars to look along with my journal. While reading the journal entry dated July 19, 2017, made no sense to me. I had written after hearing from God, "*Your heart is heavy tonight. I am with you and will help and guide you through this.*"

After reading that I said to myself, "Today is July 19, 2018. Exactly one year ago today I wrote this, what does this mean?"

I couldn't understand why I had been hearing that and seeing clearly Adam had returned home. Hearing so many different phrases and words throughout the year made me more confused. It made me think maybe my timing was off again and thought maybe it was a year later. The calendars that I had drew ended in August. I had made previous calendars starting that March of 2017. Sifting through other journal entries showed me that some things that God shared with me had happened already and some things that were still being shown to me daily still hadn't come to fruition yet.

Adam had seen me reading in my book and asked, "What are you reading?" Hesitantly I showed him the exact journal entry that I wrote to the day exactly a year later that was happening now. I explained to him I never could understand why I was hearing and seeing things and knowing he was home when I wrote them. I told him maybe I'm off a year and that you were still coming back. Adam seemed interested to keep reading in my journal. "I hope so," he said. "I am not sure if I am making the right decision."

Taking the journal and calendars from his hands, I placed them in the drawer. I couldn't see it anymore knowing that he was still leaving. I told myself that his mind was made up so that I needed to let him go. As hard as it was, I had to shut out any hope that he was coming back. We had been down this road too many times and I wasn't about to look stupid any longer.

I had phoned Felicia a few minutes later. She kept telling me that it wasn't over and that I needed to let him go. God needed to do his work. She told me to trust him and that she would be there for me through this all. Needing to hear some comforting words put me at ease.

Adam drove us to the airport. Sitting quietly not trying to cry, I looked out the window. I kept telling myself it will be okay and that God has me and has this situation under control. I knew I needed to step back. Wearing sunglasses helped disguise the tears that were welting in my eyes.

We were about halfway to the airport when he grabbed my hand and said, "If I come back, we will get you a new ring and have wedding ceremony."

Looking at him, I asked, "Why are you saying this to me now? You know I always wanted to have a wedding. This is too much pain to bare Adam, please stop." Still holding onto my hand, he repeated that he still loved me and that he didn't know what he was doing. I didn't know what to say so I said nothing to that.

Getting out of the car to change drivers, he got out and grabbed his backpack. He was too wearing sunglasses which made it easier for me to say goodbye. I knew if I looked into his deep brown eyes, I wouldn't be able to keep myself composed. Hugging me tightly, he said, "Take care and know that I do love you."

"Then don't leave. Stay and work on our marriage," was my response even though I knew he wasn't going to stay. I turned away from him and sat in the seat and drove off not even looking out of my rearview mirror.

Arriving back to my apartment, I walked in and looked around and reality hit me. I now was on my own for good. Heather and Adam no longer existed. Falling to my knees, I shouted out to God, "Why? Why is this happening all over again? Haven't I been through enough heartache and pain?"

"Please, Jesus, take this pain away. Give me your strength. I need you."

Picking myself up off from the floor, my phone began to ring. My mother was calling me. Needing to hear her voice and comfort, I was glad she had called. She gave me some good news that put a smile on my face. She had seen one of my schoolmates' friends' mother in her business. She had told her that I had written and published a book. She had acknowledged to my mother that she had seen my posting on Facebook and was excited for me. She offered to tell my mom that I could do a book signing in her store.

Not sure if I should do it as my circumstances had changed, I felt maybe my book was a lie. The book that made feel good at one time and wanting to help others now looked like it had been a joke. But then the vision that I had seen months earlier was brought back to me. I had seen books in my car traveling to Michigan. Remembering I had written this somewhere in one of my journals I went into the spare room closet where over twenty books of journals I had written since 2015 were sitting on a shelf. One advantage of having a good memory is I was good and remembering dates and months when I would journal. "Now which one did I write this in?"

"Oh yeah, it was in July of last year." Not finding it on the shelf but remembering I had just placed it in the top drawer of my dresser after showing Adam my journal entry I went to get it. Opening and turning pages to the latter part of July, there it was. I had written that I would be doing a book signing and seeing books in my car. Seeing that made me question again, "Am I a year away from everything? Look, it's the exact date that my book signing is to be held in 2018. I wrote this in 2017."

I called my friend's mom and we set up a time for my book signing. The book signing would be held in my hometown, Big Rapids, Michigan.

I called Ash and we made the plans to drive twelve hundred miles for this big event with Eastyn and Brystyn.

I didn't have any furniture to sit on except my bed so that is where I spent my night reading journal after journal until falling asleep.

Waking up the next morning, I waited for the cable guy to show up and the furniture to be delivered. Hearing the knock at the door, I was excited to see that my apartment was finally going to be furnished.

I had picked out a chair, sofa, two end tables, a coffee table, and a high-top table with four chairs for the kitchen. I even splurged and bought a stand for my television. This stand wasn't an ordinary stand. It was the type of stand that also had a built-in fake fireplace.

The day that Adam and I looked at it in the store, he was adamant about me having it. At the time I was visualizing us, watching a movie, eating popcorn, and sitting by a warm fire. The flames changed to all different colors, from blue, red, green, yellow, and white giving us various settings to set the mood to whatever we wanted.

When the gentleman unwrapped, the stand and placed it where I asked them to, it gave me a different feeling. I no longer when looking at it thought about Adam and I watching movies and eating popcorn. It was now an ordinary stand to me.

After all the furniture was brought in and placed, the men left. I sat on the couch and looked around and said, "This is now your place, Heather. You decorate it however you like."

I started hanging my crosses and pictures throughout the apartment. I refrained from putting any pictures of Adam and me up. For the first time, I was doing things the way I wanted it and not asking if it was okay. God had given me this freedom to do whatever I wanted to my apartment. I was being forced to make this my own and knowing I was single, I was able to do it the way I wanted it with no questions asked.

Working all day and into the evening, I was pleased on the progress that had been made. I decided to decorate my bathroom with owls. Owls seemed to have grown on me through the year. Looking for wisdom from God was a reminder that owls represent just that.

I still had more to decorate but I wanted to wait until after the closing of the house. Having more money to finish decorating was what I needed. The closing was just a few days away. Adam and I had discussed while he was here what each one of us would get. He was very generous in helping me to get most of our bills taken care of.

The day of the closing was here. I was happy and relieved to see it finally come to an end and a new beginning for me. God had showed me a dark-haired man and a dark-haired woman who would be buying our home, so it was no surprise to me when they walked in that is what they looked like. Another confirmation from God is what he knew I needed to keep my faith.

After the closing I knew I needed to call Adam to let him know it was completed. I was nervous in calling him as I hadn't spoken to him since the day he had left. When answering my call, he seemed cherry and happy to hear from me. I kept it brief and told him when he could expect the funds to be in our account. We had kept the same account, so it was easier for him to transfer money to me from his check.

We didn't talk that long as not much was needed to be said. I kept our conversation only business, which was hard for me. I knew he wouldn't want to hear about the pain and agony I was in.

After getting off the phone with him, I called Ash. She could tell I had been crying and upset. I didn't know that after our conversation that she in returned messaged Adam asking him to let me go for good. She told him she was tired of seeing me hurt, and not eating. She told him that I was not doing good. He told her that he was worried about me he knew that I wasn't eating and that it would take time for me to get over this. He told her to keep an eye on me and to be there for me.

TRIP TO MIDWEST

SUITCASES, BOXES WITH MY BOOKS, ASH, EASTYN, Brystyn, and myself was all packed and ready to go on our trip to Michigan. We decided to take Ash's car since her car was bigger and had more room for everyone.

We left early in the morning so the boys could sleep. While driving, Ash and I talked about stopping by the cemetery where my dad had been buried. Either one of us hadn't been back to his place since his funeral in December 2010. We had discussed many times throughout the years that we needed to go and visit his grave but never made it happen. Now with having the two boys and my dad being able not to meet them, I thought this was a good idea.

The drive to the cemetery was a little over nine hours. Ash and I switched driving back and forth, listening to all kinds of music, and had deep conversations. We have been each other's rock through it all. I now know and understand why God gave her to me at such a young age. God knew that I would need her through this hard journey that I was put on. He knew that Ash would need a younger mother so we could grow and help one another. God chooses the right parents for us. I am sure some would disagree because not all parents are good parents but through those parents God is molding us into the likeness of his son Jesus whether we know it or not. I understand bad things happen to us all, but God knows the reasons why.

She would go to church every now and then with me. The times that she would come with me, I was happy and kept praying that she would see how much that she needed Jesus in her life and that he would help her through anything she was going through.

Let's stop for a moment, and I want to ask anyone who is reading this book, "Do you think that Jesus has felt all that you have gone through in your life?" He may have not been in the same situations or circumstances, but do you feel he has felt feelings of loneliness, rejection, persecution, abandonment, shame, guilt, fear, etc.? How about when he was hanging on the cross, with blood dripping from his head, or when the slamming of the nails that were put into his hands and feet? Do you think he didn't feel all emotions that we in our lives have felt one way or another?

I wanted you to think for a moment that whatever you are going through in life, you are not alone. Jesus took away all our sins so that we could be free and to live a godly life. I am sure that while dying on the cross that Jesus felt many of these emotions. Jesus came in the flesh so he could sympathize, rejoice, comfort us whenever we needed him. He has been with you this whole time and has cried with you, laugh with you, console you, raise you and give you strength even though you may have felt you were alone. Just like his father was there with him while he was hanging on the cross.

Think about that for a moment before reading on. I had you pause for a bit so you could think back on a time in your life when things weren't going well. Did your circumstances change eventually, did you get the job you wanted, or the relationship that you had been longing for? While you were suffering, God was doing his work behind closed doors to give you what you had asked and prayed for. He hears everything and sees all.

Ash was really struggling with this third baby. She had felt she was being punished for all of her sins and kept asking me, "Mom, why does God want me to have three children? Why is it so hard?"

Being truthful with her, I answered, "I don't know, but he has chosen you for a reason and is blessing you with three children. He has a plan that you can't see yet. Embrace this gift that God has allowed you to have children. Some women would give anything to be in your shoes."

She just looked at me and shook her head and said, "Yeah, you are right. I am blessed."

We were getting closer to the exit when an overwhelming feeling from the Holy Spirit came over me. Turning down the road to my father's house to get to the cemetery, memories of all the times of traveling to see him came flooding back. The cemetery was up on a hill that overlooked his house. He had picked this place many years ago and had showed us where he was to be buried.

Eastyn was excited as he had seen "Grandpa Ron" many times. Eastyn looks a lot like my father, acts like him, and when looking at Eastyn, I could feel my dad looking back at me. I remember one time when Eastyn was about to have a birthday he would tell us that Grandpa Ron was coming. I asked him how he knew, and he would take his finger and point toward the sky.

I don't believe we give enough credit to children. They are so pure in heart and soul that if we would take the time to listen to them more you might be surprised on how much faith they really have. They remind and teach us to keep the faith no matter what.

Passing his house and seeing some changes that occurred on his property, I still had the last memory when I drove out to see him. and as I was about to leave, he had walked me out to my car and gave me the last hug that I would ever feel. Seeing him wearing his red sweatpants and red sweatshirt I could still hear him say, "Thank you for coming sweetheart, I love you, drive safe and take care." When memories come back like that I often wonder if it is a memory or if it is God bringing it back to us to comfort us as he knows how much we miss our loved ones. Almost like a sign from God to let us know that he has our loved ones with him.

Climbing up the hill in the car and then taking a turn right towards the cemetery was now in front of me. It was a warm sunny afternoon, so we parked the car and we all got out. Eastyn and Brystyn began running all around looking at flowers and decorations that were placed by many graves. Ash and I were looking for his grave site. We had seen pictures of his headstone, so we knew what we were looking for.

My father had been a carpenter like Jesus through his years. Owning his own business, he would do all kinds of carpentry and outside mowing and lawn services. His headstone had a tractor and tools engraved on the face of the headstone, along with a deer, squirrels, and birds. Every morning he would feed the animals that would come right up close to his patio. I remember sitting with my dad while he was drinking his morning coffee, staring out the sliding glass door waiting for them so he could feed them.

My heart began to beat a little faster when I heard, "I found it!" Ash screamed with excitement. The boys ran over to where their mother had been standing. I too started to jog closer to her. Kneeling to his grave tears begin to flow from my eyes. Thinking about seeing it but really being in front of it was a reality that his ashes were deep down in the ground in a wooden box.

The boys stood behind his headstone so we could take pictures. We didn't stay that long, but it was nice to finally see how his grave site looked. At the time of his death, I didn't have God in my life but now that I do, it was comforting to know that he is now with him in heaven.

We drove a while longer and then stopped at hotel to get rest. We still had ten hours or more to drive to Michigan, and everyone needed to get baths and a good night sleep.

The next morning, we got up early and continued our journey. Arriving in Michigan hours later, it was nice to have finally reached our destination. I knew that I had a big day ahead of me with my interview on the local radio show. I had to meet my friends' mother early the next morning.

That night while lying in bed, I prayed to God asking him to please take the nerves away from me and to give me the words that he wanted me to share with radio viewers. I had asked him to show me anything else and to please continue guiding me. The pain of not having Adam by my side while I was doing all with my book wasn't how I envisioned my accomplishment.

After asking God and talking to him more, he showed me that Adam was down in a pit. I could see Jesus standing from the top reaching for him to grab a hold of his hand. Adam was reaching for him but still couldn't reach Jesus's hand. The pit was dark and black. I could feel that was how Adam's soul was feeling. The flash of Loren popped into my head again. When I asked God if she was still in the picture, he showed me her name and Adam's name and then she disappeared, and Adam came walking toward me. I started feeling that Adam had been lying to me this whole time and that she was still in the picture as if she never had really left.

The next morning, my mother and I drove into town for my radio interview. With butterflies in my stomach but excited to share my book at the same time, my confidence grew, and I knew that was what God wanted me to share with the world even though Adam had stepped away again from God, me, and our marriage.

Walking into the room with the DJ and meeting others who were being interviewed eased me. I thought, "This is the time to reach out and let others know that they are not alone, and that God will always come through for us if we just follow his son Jesus along the way." My mother was present in the room which also gave me a sense of relief.

Once the interview was done, I let out a sigh of relief. "You did a great job, honey. I am so proud of you," my mother said to me, giving me a big hug.

"Thank you, I hope I made God proud. I know there was a reason for this. Thank you for coming and supporting me," I said to her, hugging her back.

Later that afternoon, my mom, Ash, and the boys met my sister at the park so we could spend time together. I was walking down by the creek by myself taking in the fresh air and the beauty that surrounded me bringing me back to the times when after school I would go and sit and listen to the water on my way to the buses. While skipping rocks in the water, a vision of Jesus and Adam came to my mind. I literally seen Jesus in the creek with Adam and he was baptizing him. I stopped for a moment to really take in the moment. These were the same visions I had seen years ago. I heard the voice of our father softly telling me to keep the faith and that he was still working on him. Clearly God was showing me that I needed to trust and believe that things weren't over for Adam and me.

I walked back to where everyone was playing in the jungle gym with the boys and shared with both my sister and mom what had just happened. Shawna who had just been baptized almost a year earlier hugged me and said, "I pray for you every day. I know how much you are hurting, and I want you to be happy." I hugged her and thanked her for not giving up on me and knowing she was supporting me along the way.

That night we decided to go see a movie. We dropped the boys off to one of my mom's friends. Her daughter was happy to babysit, which allowed us time with just the four of us: Ash, Shawna, our mother, and me. It had been a long time since we all sat and watched a movie together.

While everyone went to the concession to get candy and pop-corn, I stayed sitting in my chair in the movie theater waiting. I was looking through my emails when I saw that Adam had forwarded me a message from the management team from our apartments. "Was this a sign that God was showing me? Does this mean anything?" I really didn't need the email but that was the first time I had any communication with him since the closing date. I didn't respond to it; instead I deleted the message and put my phone away.

We all laughed during the movie and enjoyed indulging in our snacks. Family is so important. It seems as we get older, we learn to appreciate the times we can share with one another.

The next day was the day of my book signing. Being that I was still active on Facebook, I was looking forward to seeing family, friends, schoolmates, and teachers who said that they would come to my signing.

In the morning while I was slipping on a summer dress and curling my hair, I investigated the mirror and said, "No matter what, Heather, this is your day. No one is going to ruin this. You know that your story is true." I prayed that God would bring the ones who needed to be there and that I would somehow make an impact on others by sharing my testimony of faith.

When my mother and I arrived at the place of my book sign-ing, she helped me to display my books on a table. My friends from school started showing up. Greeting them with hugs and smiles, we snapped pictures to capture the moments. Answering questions and giving my testimony, they all couldn't wait to read my book. I didn't share with any of them that I and Adam were separated again. The way the book ended shared with everyone that he had returned so my book wasn't a lie. He did return but God made me purposely keep an opening for a second book. Now as I am writing this book you will all see why.

As I was signing a book, I looked up and saw my favorite teacher. She was more than just a teacher to me. She was a friend who I could confide in through my high school years. She knew a lot about me and my past and struggles with my childhood life. It was nice hearing her say how proud she was of me. No matter how old we get, it is always nice to hear that you still make your teacher proud. We visited for a while, and before she left, we took a picture together with me holding my book.

One lady who I was surprised to see was a lady who I babysat for. When I was a teenager, I would babysit three of her children on and off during the week and full time through the summer. During the week, she would attend Bible study. She had known me for years and knew how bad of a childhood I had with my step-father and she knew I was always happy to get out of my house to babysit. She stayed for a quite a while. She shared with me that she had been worried about me through the years as she would see my positings on New Age philosophy. She expressed that she would pray for me and was so happy to see that I had published a book on faith. I never knew how much I meant to her until that day. I felt so much love and gratitude toward everyone who came to my book signing.

Autographing in each book, it felt so good feeling the presence of the Holy Spirit. I was able to write the words with ease to each one knowing that they really cared and appreciated the journey that I was sharing.

An hour later, we wrapped up and before I left, I thanked my friends' mother once again for allowing me to have it at her business.

That night while getting ready for bed, I couldn't help stop thanking God for all that he had done in my life and thanked him for one of my best days of my life. I went to sleep with so much peace and joy.

Waking up on Sunday morning ready to go to church with my mother, I brought books to share with others. I was surprised on how many of her friends wanted to purchase my book. The love and support that was received outpoured all over. It felt so good doing God's work, spreading the word of his love, grace, and mercy. Being able to hear other testimonies from others who also hear and see visions from God comforted me and made me realize even more that I wasn't crazy, but that God had chosen to give me a special gift that he wanted me to share with the world.

After church, my mother and I left to spend the last day with the family. Our trip was over and now it was time to get packed up and get ready for the next morning to head back home. My mother enjoyed spending time with the boys while Ash and I packed our suitcases and loaded up the car.

While Ash was sleeping and I was driving listening to music, images began occurring to me in the sky. For the first time since Amy's death, she appeared in front of me smiling big. It was like her smile was the whole sky. Imagine yourself facing frontward. As you look straight, right in the middle of your eyes, imagine Adam standing. Then turn slightly to the right and imagine Jesus standing next to Adam which would be on your right side. Amy was standing on the other side of Adam so it would be like you see her on the left side while you face forward. So your vision would be Amy, Adam, and then Jesus.

I could hear Jesus telling me that Amy is helping him to bring Adam back the right way. Amy always had felt bad after what had happened to us in our past. I feel like she never forgave herself and this was a way that she was helping me. As the vision unfolded, I was seeing Amy putting white pants and a white shirt on Adam while Jesus was just watching her. It felt as if Jesus gave her a task to do and he was guiding her along. I wonder if that is what will happen to us once we get to heaven. Will Jesus have work for us to do for others? Like the scriptures say, "Thy will be done on Earth as it is in heaven." The vision was so strong, and I knew it was a sign that there was much more to come and that I needed to keep the faith and now seeing Amy gave me even more comfort knowing she was watching over me too.

When Ash woke up, I couldn't wait to share with her what had happened and the vision I had seen with Jesus, Adam, and Amy.

Our trip on the way home was good and once we arrived, we were happy to be back.

THE REVEAL

It was now the beginning of August 2018. I was walking down to our gym in our apartment complex. Feeling the warm sun on my face with earbuds in my ears listening to Christian music, I was ready for a good hard workout. Working out helped with my stress and it gave me time to be lifted spiritually.

Walking into the gym, I saw a lady running on the treadmill. I started on the elliptical. We both saw each other and greeted one another. As we made more conversation, she revealed to me that she was a Christian counselor. I began sharing with her my situation and asked her to pray for me. She asked me, "Have you heard of Dr. Charles Stanley, In Touch Ministries?"

I answered, "Yes, his catalogs come to my house monthly."

"Do you listen to his podcasts?" she asked.

"No, I didn't know he had any." I looked over at her.

She showed me on her phone and then took mine and downloaded the app. We continued talking about God and sharing with one another how he has showed each one of us visions and how he communicates with her. Making me feel at ease and knowing that she understood all that I was sharing with her we both began to pray for one another.

I love seeing how God works in our lives. He brings in the people who will help us grow spiritually at the right time. He knew that I needed to meet others who walk in the faith just as I.

After they gym, I went back to the apartment and started listening to podcast after podcast. While listening to him, I journaled and took notes on his sermons. His voice soothed me and made me feel closer to God than I had ever before. His words of wisdom and encouragement gave me so much strength.

Later that evening, I was getting a sense that Adam was changing his truck insurance. I don't know why but I felt something was happening. A vision came to me. It was a new truck with Texas license plates on it. Feeling uneasy about it, I looked in my phone for any emails indicating that there was a change to our policy. We had kept all business the same once he left. Seeing that there was a change in our policy, and it was the weekend, I knew I couldn't call until Monday to find out what was going on. "Heather, it isn't any of your business. He's gone. Let him go." Then I saw Loren in his new truck. That was the moment that God revealed to me that she was still in the picture and that Adam had lied about everything. He had always had her and it was his plan all along to sell the house, move me, and he would start his new life with her.

"Thank you, God, now what do you want me to do?" I was so angry. I really had thought that he wanted to be on his own and that she had been out of the picture but now seeing the whole year that he was here he was still playing me.

I waited until Monday morning to call him. Walking around the apartment nervous, angry, hurt, holding my phone I began dialing his number. When he answered his words right away, "Before you say anything, I don't know what I am doing? I am lost and things are not the same. We will never be over."

My response to him was, "I know you are still with her. I have seen her around you. You never left her. I have been a joke to you this whole time. I know you bought a truck, and let me guess, it's maroon, right?"

"How do you know what color it is?"

"Adam, I have told you over the years that God shows me everything. I had seen a maroon truck in 2015 for you. I was right when you bought a white one too. Don't you get it? God speaks to me and has given me this special gift. I don't know why because the pain is so hard now knowing that she was still in the picture this whole time. I really believed you when you left this time telling me that you needed to be on your own to find yourself. Now I know why you said what you did. You never even tried with us this whole last year. You can't have your cake and eat it too."

"I am sorry, but this time it's different. It's not the same," he told me.

"What do you mean? Do you want to come home?"

Waiting for his response, he once said again, "Yes, but the right way. I thought when I left I would be able to get you out of my mind, but I think about you every day."

Of course, hearing that made me feel good and relieved to hear that he still had feelings for me. "I told you, Adam, we are connected more than you ever know. I really feel like you thought you could just leave but what you didn't realize is that my soul went with you. We can't work on our marriage if you are still with her. I really think my timing is off and God has always been working on us through the years."

"Yeah, you are right," he stated.

We talked for over an hour and once again I thought maybe all that I said really did get through to him and he would be on his way back home to fix us. His conversation gave me so much hope. I had tried turning off my feelings from him once he left, but once he told me that he still loved me, it opened my heart up all over again.

I had asked him when he was coming to town and he said that it would be the first part of September to get his plates for his black work truck. When he had come home that previous June, he had purchased a black truck and he had been waiting for the tags. When trying to get his tags the truck hadn't been registered in the system and wasn't available. Isn't it interesting how God arranges circumstances to give us glimpses of his master plans? There are no coincidences or accidents in our lives. God knows every detail of every moment of each and everyone's lives.

Hanging up the phone, he said he still loved me and to please keep doing what I had been doing, which was praying and listening to God.

My life looked a little merrier than before and looked more hopeful to me. I continued listening to Dr. Stanley to keep my strength. I learned so much from him. There was a sermon on "God's Timing" that really helped me to see how God works in each other's lives.

I had to see that God always doesn't bring us what we ask for if the timing isn't right. God still must need things to happen in our lives. He needs to put us through other circumstances so that he can continue cleaning our souls. He puts us in situations that are uncomfortable so that our soul can grow and that it isn't on our timing. Not wanting to hear that but knew it was true, I also started seeing how God was getting me ready for the next few months. There was yet so much more that needed to happen for me to really surrender to him.

I listened to that podcast over and over to help me stay focus on his work and continued trusting him.

One night while I was watching television, I could feel that Kitty was going to be calling me soon. I hadn't spoken to her since Adam had left and she knew nothing of what had changed in our relationship. I didn't want to alarm her as we had plans coming up. I had overseen preparing the itinerary for lodging for the wedding in November. I thought since it was still months away that things might change by then. I had told her months before that we would use our timeshare to stay in Las Vegas so there would be no expense.

I kept a lot to myself. It was different for me this time. I didn't want his family involved as I felt it was Adam's place to tell all.

A couple of days later as I was sitting reading, my phone rang. Looking down to see who was on the face of my phone, there it was, Kitty. "What am I to say?" Answering it hesitantly, I changed my tone right away. She had called to let me know that she needed our new address so she could send out Adam's birthday card. Keeping our conversation light, I didn't divulge where he was now and living. I didn't feel good not telling her the truth, but I just couldn't bare talking about it and I was still hoping that things may change, and we would be back together. I didn't want to talk bad anymore about her son. Especially after our conversation earlier in the month that

Adam and I had. Our conversation gave me so much hope to continue keeping the Faith.

Adam's fiftieth birthday was a few days away. God had been telling me that I couldn't reach out to him and that he needed to feel the absence of me. In the past four years of our separation, I had always reached out to him even while he was still with Loren.

God brought back a thought to me that I had thought in 2016 that I will never forget. I was standing in the kitchen by the coffee area when God showed me that Adam would be fifty years old before the sin was out of him. "I can't and won't wait that long. That's still two years away. No way." I remember saying out loud and ignoring the thought and feeling.

Looking at where I am now, never thinking I would be in the same position, and knowing he was about to turn fifty made me see that back then God was giving me a glimpse of what was yet to come.

The power of God is so strong. He knew where I would be two years later. I began to realize more so that he knows where we will be in one minute, one second, one hour, one year, etc. He knows all.

I had become stronger throughout the years since having Jesus as my personal savior. Jesus was now walking beside me each day and guiding me as this season in my life was so uncertain. God knew I needed to draw more strength through his son so I could continue the walk through the darkness. Jesus was my light and I needed to keep following him.

It took all the strength on his day not to reach out to him. Keeping busy helped me not to think that he was celebrating this special birthday. That night God had told me he was proud of me for not reaching out. I could feel the wrath and anger of God in my room. Clearly, he said to me, "I am going to go get my son. This is enough." I was on the phone with Felicia when I was hearing this, and she shared with me that it was going to get harder before it would get better.

A few days later, I was surfing the channels and movies on television and came across the movie *Fireproof*. Years ago, one of my friends at the bowling alley had asked me if I had ever seen the movie.

He had recommended to me then, but I never took the time to watch it.

I stopped for a moment and then realized that was the movie that he had spoken to me about. With my dog Gracee lying next to me, I began watching it. The movie reminded me of Adam. The character played by Kirk Cameron reminded me of how greedy Adam was and how he only had only thought of himself and his needs. In the movie, Kirk was complaining to his colleagues about his marriage how it was dull, and he didn't know if he wanted to be in it. He wasn't sure if he wanted to put the effort in anymore.

The woman who played his wife reminded me of myself at times. She was a type of wife who wanted attention from her husband but tended to nag at times asking him to do things for her and to be present in their marriage. She would ask him to take her on dates, but Kirk was too busy to hear his wife's needs.

There was a part in the movie that moved me to reach out to Adam via an email. Marriage is like the movie *Fireproof*. If a fire gets too big and needs to be contained, we need water to put it out, so it doesn't continue spreading.

In every beginning of a relationship, there is lust, excitement, giddiness, and all of us trying to be on our best behavior. After the honeymoon period is over, the real person comes to surface. Little things that we thought were cute in the beginning, we now find annoying. Our spouses forget that the relationship needs water to grow. Just like in a fire, if the flames get to big and out of our control, we know that water will put out the fire.

The water represents having Jesus in our lives. He needs to be the center of anyone's marriage. He is the one who makes sure that the fire doesn't get out of control and if he sees us going in the wrong direction, he will put the fire out on his own time.

After being married for years, we all get to comfortable in our lives and our lives become complacent. Marriage takes work, dedication, devotion, love, trust, and honesty. Keeping the marriage alive requires both parties, not just one but two.

Jesus is our helper when we find ourselves falling away from righteousness. The devil likes to see families break up. He likes to put shiny new things in front of our lives. He likes to play with our minds. He is lurking around even when we don't think he is there just waiting to prey on the weak.

Having Jesus in our lives daily and being devoted to him and letting him guide you helps keep the devil away. Your thoughts are different, you look at life differently and you keep yourself held accountable of your actions.

There was a song in the movie called "While I'm Waiting" sung by John Waller that really grabbed my attention. I went to my phone and downloaded the song and lyrics. I listened to that song over and over really listening to the words. I could see how Jesus was there with me while I was waiting for God to show me what he was doing with me, Adam, and my marriage.

In my email, I expressed and begged Adam to download and to watch the movie. I asked him to please ask himself if he did everything he could to work on our marriage and if he did to please let me go so I could find a marriage that I deserved.

Waking up the next morning hoping to have received a response from him but finding no email disappointed me. I got dressed and went to the gym to listen to my daily podcast. The podcast was about sin and how to overcome the addiction by letting Jesus be your savior. When listening to it, God whispered to me to share with him. "Why? He never responds to anything I share with him. He doesn't care. It's a waste of my time," I pleaded to God.

"Just do it. You will see."

I felt I was fighting back and forth with God, but in the end, I knew I needed to obey and trust him. So, after the podcast was finished, I shared it in Adam's email.

It was September sixth and I was over to Ash's apartment watching the boys. While I was sitting on the couch watching a children's movie with them, God had me look over to her front door. There I saw Adam standing in the entrance, smiling and happy to see us all. I couldn't understand why I was seeing that vision as Adam had never been to her new apartment. I heard the words, "Trust me. You will see."

After Ash returned home, I went back home to journal. While I was scrolling through on Pinterest, I came across something that was very helpful to me to help me to discern the voice of God or Satan. I am sure others like me asked this question before. "How do I know if it's God's voice I am hearing or if it's Satan's voice?" Well, let me share with you this posting and then you will know for sure.

God's Voice	*Satan's Voice*
Stills you	Rushes you
Leads you	Pushes you
Reassures you	Frightens you
Enlightens you	Confuses you
Encourages you	Discourages you
Comforts you	Worries you
Calms you	Obsesses you
Convicts you	Condemns you

God is never early and he's never late. He's always right on time and his plans for you are good.

God is a God of love and order. If the voice you are hearing doesn't sound like those things, then they are not from him. It's that simple. Whenever God speaks to me now, it is easier for me to trust him by referring to the feelings he gives me when he speaks.

Before I was about to doze off, I got the sense that Loren was angry about something. I could feel that she was not happy with Adam but didn't know why.

In the middle of the night, I was awaken by hearing Adam's voice saying to me, "I want to see you. I need to see you. I am on my way." Feeling like he was in his truck heading this way, I sat up and reached for my phone to see if I could see if he had spent any money to give me an indication that he was on his way. Seeing that he had stopped off to a gas station that was on the path toward Colorado, I was sure that he was near. It had been fifty-four days since we saw each other. I couldn't help but think that I was really going to see him.

I tried going back to sleep but couldn't. I anticipated our conversation if I was to see him. After finally being able to get some more sleep, I woke up and got myself ready. I was going over to Ash's apartment to babysit the boys.

When I arrived to her place, I had told her I thought that he was on his way but wasn't for sure. I told her if I was late getting to work that would be the reason why.

As the morning grew on, there was still no message, no phone call from Adam. "Maybe he doesn't want to see me after all." After thinking that the feeling didn't seem true, so I set aside my pride and reached out to him. I told him I knew he was in town and asked if he wanted to see me. He answered yes, a few moments later asking me where I was. I gave him Ash's address.

As I await with sweaty palms, my heart beating fast, looking into the mirror to make sure myself looked good, I heard a knock on the door. The boys were playing in their room when Eastyn ran to the door to answer it. He was so happy to see his grandpa. Brystyn wasn't too far behind Eastyn to greet him. Adam knelt and gave both boys a big hug and held onto to them tightly for moments.

I walked over to him and he reached his arms out for me and he gave me the longest hug I think I have ever received from him. I could feel his soul connect with mine and it gave me such a warm peaceful feeling. I refrained from any kissing but felt comfortable in hugging him.

Eastyn reached for his hand and led him into his bedroom so he could show him his new bed that I had bought for him. Both boys shared a room, so it made sense in purchasing bunk beds. Eastyn was proud and excited to show his grandpa that he could put the ladder next to the bed to climb to the top. Smiling and looking at Grandpa, he said, "See, Grandpa, I am a big boy now."

"Yes, you are, good job," was his response.

While the boys were playing, Adam and I had a chance to talk. I asked him if he had listened to what I sent him. He looked into my eyes and said, "Yes, it is helping me to see things differently." Shocked to hear him say that as he always scoffed at any time, I would speak about God made me see and realize something little was changing in him.

He told me that he believed in my visions and that he knew I could hear God. For the first time, I didn't feel crazy and that it was comforting to know that he believed.

I wanted to ask so many questions, but I knew I wouldn't get the answers that I needed so I made our conversation light. At one point, he asked if he could go to the apartment and get a few things that he needed. As I gave him the key, he added, "I will let Gracee out to while I am there. I will be back."

"Okay, thank you."

"The apartment looks good. You decorated it nicely," he said walking in thirty minutes later.

"Thanks. I changed a few things and wanted my apartment to represent me and made it my own."

I had shared with him that the south salon was now officially CC's. The changeover happened the first of September. He seemed pleased to hear that we were now back to one salon.

The tags still weren't ready to be picked up so he said that the DMV would let him know once they arrived.

He wanted me to see his new truck. As we were walking out to where his truck was parked, he reached for my hand. Seeing his truck from a distance, I said, "This is a nice color. This is beautiful." He opened the driver's side so I could peek in. He sat there and just looked at me.

I asked him if he even noticed that I didn't reach out to him on his birthday. "Yes, I thought maybe you would but understood why you didn't. It felt different not hearing from you. That is for sure." I told him I wanted to, but God held me back and I knew I needed to listen to him.

I had remembered his mom's birthday card came in the mail. I had kept it in my glove box, so I walked over to my car to get it out. Handing it to him, he opened and saw that she had given him a gift card to a restaurant. "Here, you take it. I won't use it," he said, handing to me.

My quick response was, "Oh yeah, you can't let her see it then. She will know we saw each other. I get it." I took it out of his hand abruptly. I am sure he felt my anger at that moment.

I had asked if Loren was mad knowing he was coming here today. I explained that I could feel her angry yesterday. He looked at me and said, "Yes, she was mad, but she will get over it."

"I knew it," I said, and also sharing with him the vision I had seen the day before his arrival that he would be standing in Ash's apartment giving me a hug.

"I better get going. I have a long drive ahead." The words I didn't want to hear.

"Yep, you do. It was nice seeing you. Thanks for stopping by," is all I could say to him.

He added, "Please eat, you are too thin, and I worry about you."

"Don't worry about me. I will be fine."

With tears welting up in my eyes knowing he was leaving to go back to Texas, he took his hand and wiped my tears and said, "Well, now I can't say that I am not coming back."

Looking at him, I asked, "So you do have feelings for me still?"

"Yes, I need to work on me. I needed to see you. I want to come back one hundred percent."

I didn't know what to say after hearing that because the reality was, he was still choosing to leave once again. I turned and walked away without looking back.

Walking back into the apartment and reflecting on our conversation I asked God, "Is he coming back?" The same response was given to me. "He's not coming back the same. Back in a flash."

Trying to finish the day in the salon was hard and emotional. Rehearsing every conversation, every look, and every thought kept playing in my mind.

When walking into my apartment my apartment didn't feel so lonely anymore. It was like I could feel Adam's energy in here even though he wasn't here. It felt as if it wasn't just my apartment. "Hmm, this feels weird and strange but good," I thought to myself walking into my bedroom. After putting my night clothes on I walked into the closets and reached on the shelf a journal from September 2017. Amazed to see what I had written on September seventh. The entry stated that when seeing Adam that he would be different and that his hug would be warm and more loving. "I must be off a year. Today is September seventh." God knew my heart was heavy and I needed the glimpse that God was still working on our situation.

I rested well that night and prayed and thanked God for the day he had given me.

Getting ready for work the next morning, while brushing my teeth, a sense came over me to look in the file box to make sure that nothing was taken out while Adam was here. When opening and seeing that his passport was gone my heart sank. "No, why did he take it? Is he taking her on a trip or on our trip?" Fear came rushing back and all bad thoughts poured in like a freight train. At that moment I didn't care, I needed to call Adam and ask him why he took it.

I calmed myself first and knew that I couldn't come across harsh. When he answered I worked around the question that I was dying to ask. "Is there a reason why you took your passport? Are you going on a trip?" Surprised that he didn't seem mad that I asked, his response, "No, I needed another form of ID for my renewal for my CDL license."

"Oh, okay, that's a relief to me. I am sorry but it freaked me out. I know we really didn't talk yesterday about our Paris trip and I thought maybe you were taking her and didn't want to tell me."

I expressed to him what I had found in my journal that night after I was home and again told him that I think my timing was off. Our conversation was short but felt better, and when he again told me he loved me, it reassured me that we were not over.

Stopping by the mailboxes to check my mail on my way into the complex, I sat in my car looking through the letters. Seeing an envelope for a travel company addressed to Adam, I opened it. My hands were shaking wondering what was in it. Seeing it was a voucher with a two night stay in Las Vegas, the thought came to my mind that he was planning on taking Loren to Daxx's wedding instead of me.

Right away I called my mother in tears explaining to her what had happened in finding that his passport was taken and now seeing a voucher I knew something was stirring. Either he was taking her out of the country, or she was going to the wedding or both. I knew God was sharing with me what was coming that there had been a reason why he wanted to go to the apartment by himself. "He is so sneaky, Mom. How could he?" My mother was trying to calm me down, but I was livid, upset, and felt like an idiot.

From that point on, I knew he wasn't coming back anytime soon and that I had let him suck me back into his games all over again.

Keeping myself busy in the salon and redirecting my life in a new direction the thought of us getting back together begin to dissipate.

About a week later Wednesday, I was looking at our bank account and noticed he was traveling back this way. "That's weird, usually I would hear his voice asking to see me. I wonder why this time it;s different?" Then I saw Loren's face smiling and laughing which told me he wasn't coming alone. I couldn't help myself. I needed to see if what I was seeing was true, so I texted him asking if he was here and if so, asking if I was going to see him. I really wanted to ask him about the travel voucher but wanted to do it face-to-face. A half hour later he responded explaining that the tags were in and that his mouthpiece had cracked and was in Colorado Springs replacing it. When I asked again if I was going to see him, he told me he was sorry, but he couldn't. I knew then that she was with him. The wrath in me just exploded. I messaged back and said horrible things that couldn't be helped.

I was fighting with myself all over again letting the devil work his way back into my thoughts and feelings. I was trying so hard to move on, but it was very hard hearing and seeing visions that God was showing me.

FIFTEEN YEARS

WE WERE CELEBRATING ASH'S BIRTHDAY WHEN MY phone rang. Seeing it was Adam, I handed her my phone without even answering it. I had nothing to say to him and needed to stay strong after what happened. It had been weeks since our last conversation, and with each passing day, I was letting Adam go. In their conversation, he had told her to tell me hi and that he had hoped I was doing good and if I needed anything to "please let him know."

That evening after her birthday, Adam reached via text to me asking me how I was doing. I never really like texting, so I called him instead. The reception was bad, that we kept getting disconnected forcing us to text instead.

He had shared with me that Lisa, the first woman who he had an affair with, reached out to him letting him know that she had just finished reading my first book. She eluded to him that she wanted to see him. He told me that he wasn't even thinking about visiting her and that he was taken time for him.

At one point in our texting back and forth, he brought up and idea that maybe we should get divorced so then we could start over. When reading that crushed me to think that we would have to divorce to start over. In asking him if it would just be him and me dating, he couldn't be sure. Seeing that message come through didn't make me feel good, instead making me think this was just a game to him so that he wouldn't feel guilty anymore on how he was living his life. He told me he knew that he couldn't see me out of his life but knew too much damage had been done. I didn't respond anymore to him after that.

We were in our slow season, so finances were a little tight for my needs. I had reached out asking him if I could have a little more money. Our conversation started good but when asked about us and where we were headed the conversation turned another direction. We started texting back and forth hurtful words when in the end, he told me was blocking me and deleting me from his Facebook.

Something shifted within me after that. I felt like he had just cut me off completely and that he had made his choice once and for all.

Reading scriptures and writing in my journal God started floating divorce papers in the air around me. Getting my attention, I asked him, "Are we divorcing?"

Immediately the papers would fall to the ground in shredded pieces and the words NO DIVORCE appeared.

After seeing that I decided to call and set up a time with the same lawyer, I had called back in 2015. The date was set for a week later. The first time I had went, God wasn't present in my life. I remember feeling frightened. This time felt different as I knew Jesus was walking with me. As I sat and waited for my appointment, God told me to read in Corinthians. I turned to the pages of marriage and strength that he knew I needed. I prayed before going in and that I knew I wasn't alone.

The gentleman had remembered me which was nice. We sat down and he showed me all the figures and obligations that Adam would have to provide for me if we were to divorce. Looking at the figures and seeing what would be paid out to me gave me relief knowing that I would be taken care of and that for the last fourteen years of our marriage, and all the pain I had been put through, God would make sure that I would be taken care.

The lawyer also expressed how much his costs were, and to me, the fees were too steep. He had told me that the divorce could be final in ninety days from the day that Adam would be served. Thanking him for his time, I told him I would think about it and get back with him. Getting into the car, I felt frustrated as I knew I didn't have his retainer fee so he could begin the process.

On the way home, as I was talking to God, he reassured me that it would be okay and that he had this under control. All I needed to do was keep the faith.

Waking up the next morning was now October 1, 2018. My fifteen-year anniversary was just a day away. While I was working and cleaning a bed, God told me that he would be reaching out to me on our anniversary, but he asked me not to respond to him. I promised God that if he did, I would not respond back.

I was sitting in the chair at my desk writing in my journal when God flashed me Daxx's wedding. I again saw my grandson Owen meeting Loren, and I saw Big Ashley and her dad arguing. I started feeling his mom and dad angry and turning Adam away. The first thing that came back to me was a vision I had seen in May 2017. I remember seeing Adam and Loren getting dressed up and going to a wedding or formal evening. I then remembered that after the function, Adam had decided to leave Loren for good and he came back home to me.

Seeing that vision and knowing clearly again, I knew that Adam was going to take Loren to Daxx's wedding. What God also showed me was a lot of arguing and fighting between them including Adam and Loren. I saw Loren angry that she wouldn't be able to attend the actual wedding. I saw like pieces of a church falling on her head while she was holding on to Adam's hand. Before pieces of the debris would hit Adam, I had seen him letting go her hand just in time.

When seeing this vision, I was surprised on how I reacted. I feel like God was preparing me early on that this was part of his plan and that this was the time that this vision was coming true. My mind started accepting that Adam had chosen Loren and that his life was now completely with her as he was about to introduce his whole family to her. I knew then that there was no place for me in his or his children's lives.

After returning home from work, I looked for the journal that had showed that vision years ago to me. As I read it, I could see that this was what God was preparing me for. I knelt on the floor looking

116

at Jesus's picture and asked him to please help me get through this and to show me how I could serve him papers.

As I was praying, my phone began to ring. I saw that it was Kitty calling. I wanted to talk to her as it had been a few months since we last spoke. She and I spoke for hours. After Adam and I had our last fight, he called his mom to let her know that he had left me. Kitty had been upset and didn't know what to say to me, so she left me alone but for some reason that night, she was feeling like she needed to reach out to me. I shared with her the vision that I was seeing and prepared her to get ready to meet Loren.

She already knew that she would be coming along as she had spoken to Big Ashley and both could tell by the way Adam was acting that she was coming whether they liked it or not. Adam made it clear that he would do what he wanted without being questioned nor care about what anyone had felt about the situation.

Kitty told me that she didn't and wouldn't meet her because it was so wrong as to what Adam was planning. Adam and I weren't even legally separated, and Dan and Kitty knew that I didn't deserve to be treated this way, and since he was still married to me, they had no intentions of meeting her and disrespecting me.

It was a relief to hear that Dan and Kitty was standing beside me while I was going through all the pain and heartache. I gave her the itinerary information so she would be able to get her room without any complications. She thanked me and told me to hang in there and to keep praying.

The next day, I woke up to a fifteen-year anniversary alone. I had gone over to Ash's apartment to watch the boys. Watching television with the boys and playing helped keep me preoccupied. While we were playing, I heard a chime from my phone, letting me know that I had received a text. Moments before then, God had spoken to me again telling me not to respond, assuring God that I would obey him.

Walking into the living room to retrieve my phone that was face down lying on the table, I picked it up. Turning it over and seeing it was Adam who messaged me. Reading the words Happy Anniversary. Expressing that he was sorry that this was the way this year had turned out for us. He told me that he thinks of me every day and wanted me to know.

As I read that there, were no feelings of excitement within me. For the first time, my attitude was different knowing that they were just words of guilt and nothing more. Just like I promised God, I did not respond.

The month of October had just begun. I had my good days and bad days. Some days I would cry and other days I cared about nothing. Pushing on staying in my faith was strengthening me through the darkness of my life. I had joined on Thursday morning's a Bible study in our church. The women whom I met were very warm and loving toward me. Each of them began to pray for me and my marriage. Being around strong women of faith helped me to stay focus on God's bigger plan for my life.

A few days later, I had spoken to Adam regarding business. We talked for a few minutes and then I asked him if he was taking Loren to the wedding and if he had decided if she is who he wanted to spend the rest of his life with. He told me that is what he was trying to figure out. I asked him point blank if he wanted a divorce and he told me he didn't want that. Our conversation was going nowhere so I ended it quickly.

As the month went on, I continued praying to God. He reassured me that things were going to be okay and that I needed to listen and follow him.

In the middle of the month, Ash and I went to her doctor's appointment and found out that she was having another boy. She had hoped it was going to be a girl but when we had seen the 3D sonogram and saw the new human growing inside of her, we were excited to see a healthy baby.

Earlier in the year, we had bought great deals on baby items when the closing of Babies R Us happened. We really didn't buy any clothes since we were unsure of the gender. After we left the appointment, we went to other stores to buy clothes now knowing it was a boy.

Getting home with all the new clothes we had purchased; Ash was feeling better about the change that was coming in a few short

months. Having a weird feeling that made me worry about her pregnancy, I couldn't help to think something was going to go wrong.
God started showing me that while we were in the hospital I was
going to be in different rooms. I saw myself moving from place to
place in a panic. In one vision, he even showed that Adam was around
which made no sense to me. "Is he going to be here by then God?" I
asked. God then showed me the same vision once again.

The Awakening Begins

IT WAS NOW THE MONTH OF NOVEMBER, the month that I really didn't want to face. The wedding was drawing near. I stayed steadfast in my daily devotions and read the Bible to keep me walking in the faith.

I had come across this that became a part of my morning and nightly prayer:

Prayer Changes Everything

A primary purpose of prayer is to discover the Lord's will for our lives. As we seek *His* way, He works in our hearts and minds to guide us with *His* word and develop our understanding of the situation. Then our eyes will be opened to *His* point of view so we can pray according to *His* will. And when we pray for *His* will to be done in *His* timing, we will be amazed at what *He* can accomplish.

To simplify this prayer, I began saying, "Your will is my will, Lord" That became my mantra whenever I started questioning or felt afraid, worried, or any emotion that arose within me.

It's true, God already knows what, where, and who will be in our lives. He knew the work that needed to be done so that we could honor his son Jesus Christ.

Waking up that Friday morning, the weekend of the wedding, I could feel the unsettledness from Adam's parents. I could even see the arguments that were about to happen between Big Ashley and her dad. I had seen Big Ashley crying and her son not happy. The air felt heavy and dark.

All weekend visions were coming in. On Sunday morning, the day of the wedding, I woke up seeing a bomb hitting Adam while he was standing in the wedding party during the ceremony. I saw a snake slithering around the bride, and I saw Loren angry. Seeing her sitting and sulking. I thought, "I wonder if she is able to go to the actual wedding or is she even allowed to attend?"

I went on my day and attended church. During the service as I was praying to God to please show me what his will was for me, divorce papers appeared again. When I would ask the same question whether we would divorce, God would crumble the papers and they would disappear. I was trying so hard to understand what he was trying to show me.

A few days later, Kitty called me on the way to work. I parked my car so we could talk without any distractions. She shared with me that the weekend had been horrible. Adam tried to get his mom and dad to meet Loren but they both refused, and his dad told Adam at one point that he knew it was wrong in what he was doing.

Kitty was so upset seeing Big Ashley and Owen hurt by Adam. Apparently Big Ashley and her dad got into a fight and left Big Ashley in tears. Owen who had been excited to see his grandpa was uncomfortable when he had to meet Loren.

I had asked her if Loren could attend the wedding. Kitty answered back angrily, "Absolutely not!" She wasn't going to allow that as it was a disgrace to me and to his parents.

We talked awhile longer and then hung up. "See, I know this is what God was showing and telling me. Heather, you have to keep the faith." Everything I had seen back May 2017 had happened.

On a Friday night in the gym while I was running on the treadmill, God showed me a new vision. Adam was walking toward me, but from a distance, he was crying.

"God, why is he crying?" I asked.

Then as Adam's face came closer to me. He was holding up and ripping divorce papers saying, "I don't want a divorce, please forgive me."

Seeing that vision for the first time, I asked God, "Do you want me to get divorce papers?"

"Yes," he replied loudly.

"Okay, I will. I trust you and if this is your will, it is my will." Still running on the treadmill and not wanting to do what our Father asked, I could feel the Holy Spirit pushing me to listen to what I was instructed to do.

God had made me feel that finally the awakening had begun. My eyes were clearly opened and knowing that Adam took her to my step-son's wedding, it was crystal clear to me that our marriage was over, and it was time for me to move on.

Walking in from my long work out and feeling relieved, I called Kitty to let her know what I was going to do. "You really have no other choice at this point," she said to me. "I am sorry you are going through this but this what he wants. Once he brought her to the wedding, it was clear to me that he is done with you."

I couldn't help but cry but told her that I would always be here for her and thanked her for our relationship. We had a rocky start from the beginning, but over the years, she and I became close. She pushed me to follow Jesus and she helped saved me. I would be forever grateful for her. I told her that I did all that I could do to save my marriage, but I couldn't do it anymore.

The next day one of our clients came into the salon who had been a great friend over the years. She knew what I had been going through, so when I told her what I was going to do, she offered to go with me to the courthouse. She knew more about the process than I did. We agreed for her to come to my place that Monday morning and we would go.

Over the weekend, I had written up documents stating what I wanted in the divorce. The process allowed us to go to mediation if Adam and I didn't agree. The more God made me write, the stronger I had become and the only thing that mattered now was that I was set free to live my life. I no longer had anymore thoughts of Adam and me getting back together. My new life was now my own, and I knew if Jesus was by my side walking with me, I could get through anything.

Monday morning, we were headed down to the courthouse. The last time I had been down to the courthouse was when Adam and I said, "I do." Feeling nauseous and sick to my stomach as we arrived, before getting out of the car, we both prayed.

Walking up to the counter, I asked the lady for a packet to file for divorce. God kept saying to me, "You do this. I take it from here." In handing me the packet, she explained on how the process worked and how long it would take for the divorce to go through.

Driving back with my friend, we stopped off to a copier place and made three copies.

She dropped me off hugging me and telling me that it will be okay and if it is God's will, he will let the divorce go through.

Walking in, I laid the packet on the table and went straight to my room, knelt, and looked at my picture of Jesus. "Okay, I did what you asked me to do, now what? Please guide me. I am listening to you." I stayed silent so I could hear him.

"Fill out the papers and then put in your top drawer when finished."

I got up and grabbed a pencil and pen and went out to the dining area and sat in the chair. With a pencil, I went through the whole packet filling out all the necessary details. When finished I looked it over and felt confident that it was correct. I then took another copy and filled out with ink. After finishing, I picked up the papers and put back in the packet and placed in my top drawer of the dresser.

"Now it's done, I need to get him here so he can be served. What is next?"

Nothing came from God, so I knew it wasn't time for me to know anything else.

I feel like sometimes God stretches us in his own way to grow our souls. He knows how hard to stretch us and when to stretch us. Trusting him and learning to completely surrender to him was what I was facing.

I went to the gym to work out and listen to Charles Stanley. Knowing what I needed to do, I still prayed for Adam's soul to be saved regardless if I was in his life or not. God had me share other podcasts with him to let him know that I was still in his life for a reason. I now could look at Adam as just Adam without adding any titles to his name.

As I was working out, God was showing me a Turkey. This turkey wasn't sitting on a plate ready to be served, it was like flying across the table. Thanksgiving was right around the corner, so I wasn't sure what that meant but I knew it meant something.

A day before Thanksgiving, I was sitting in my chair reading and writing when my phone chimed in with a message. Looking down, it was Adam reaching out to me. He wished me a Happy Thanksgiving and told me what I had been sending him was helping him more and more each day. Responding back, I let him know that I was glad to hear. I told him that I pray for him each day and that he would be free from all his sin.

Asking God, "Is this the time to ask him to come into town, so he can be served?"

Hearing right away, "Not yet, it's coming. Be patient."

"Okay, I will."

I asked Adam if I could share something else with him and he responded back "absolutely." So I began to really message him asking him to surrender his life to Jesus and to make him his center and that he would guide you in the right direction. I stressed to him the importance of having Jesus in your life every day.

I kept it brief but to the point that I knew he would understand. He messaged back one last time thanking me again.

The next day, Ash and the boys came over for Thanksgiving dinner. I must admit our turkey didn't turn out the way I thought it would. We had bought Cornish hens since it was just us. We laughed when we opened the oven and saw that after four hours of cooking, it still wasn't done. All the other fixings were ready to eat so we had a Thanksgiving dinner minus the main course.

Our tradition after having Thanksgiving was to decorate the Christmas tree. While Ash was cleaning up the dishes, I went out to the garage and opened the garage to get better lighting to bring in the Christmas tree and boxes. Without being aware that Gracee our dog followed me out, she ran out of the garage. Luckily, I saw her little white tail out of the corner of my eye and yelled, "Gracee, get back in here right now." She looked up at me from running and turned around and high tailed her butt back in. As I turned to open the door back into the apartment, God softly said, "December second." Hmm wonder what that means.

Earlier in the week, I had went over to Felicia's house and while we were looking through her Christmas decorations, she asked if I wanted to borrow some. I really didn't want to put anything up that reminded me of our previous Christmas's as the life I knew was fading away. I was excited that she offered, and I accepted her offer of kindness. We loaded a few tubs and placed in the back of my car.

Ash and I started unpacking the Christmas tree to set it up. We put on Christmas music to listen to while decorating. The boys wrapped themselves in tinsel dancing and twirling around laughing. The Christmas spirit was filled in my apartment.

Later, Ash went home with her boys to decorate their first Christmas tree in their new apartment. She had taken quite a bit of my old decorations to use for her place.

I finished decorating each bathroom, the hallway, my room, and the entry way. My apartment felt warm and cozy. I put on a Christmas movie and sat down to relax. While watching the movie, I heard, "Back in a flash."

Happy to see November ending, I felt strong and was ready to turn my life toward a new direction.

It was now December second. I had just finished closing the salon and was heading home. Walking into the apartment, I could hear Gracee crying to get out of her kennel. She had been in all day and knew she had to go the bathroom. After living in my apartment for a few months and seeing that Gracee had to be kenneled more and couldn't run and be free, I knew that I needed to do something with her. I felt bad leaving her all alone. Animals need a lot of love and attention, and I knew I wasn't the right owner for her.

I took her out of the kennel and walked her around the complex. It began to start snowing so I brought her in.

Earlier in the day, I had decided that this was the night that I would pack up all of Adams things to put into tubs and store in garage until he came into town. I had stopped on my way home to Target to purchase the tubs.

While Gracee was lying on my bed, I was in my closet taking out Adam's clothes and throwing them onto the bed. Gracee looked at me and I said, "Your dad isn't coming back so I am packing up his things." Gracee turned her head like she was listening to me. She smelled his clothes as I was throwing them on the bed. She quickly jumped off my bed and ran out to the living room. I followed her and when I walked into the living room, I found her curled up on the couch laying on a blanket sulking. Thinking and asking to myself, "Does she really know that he's not coming back?" Walking over to her I sat down to pet her and told her that I loved her and that I was sorry for all that she had been through. She laid looking at me.

I went back into the room to answer my phone as it was ringing. It was Ash letting me know that she was on her way over to help me.

When she arrived, I was moving the tubs around in the garage to make more room for Adam's tubs. I was separating my things from his to make it easier for him to grab and go. The boys ran into the house to watch television while Ash and I worked in the garage.

About thirty minutes went by and Ash went into the house as the snow was now coming down hard and sticking to the ground. Ash came out to the garage moments later and asked, "Where is your dog?"

"She's in the house lying on the couch," I answered back.

"No, she's not."

"Well, maybe she is lying on my bed, I don't know. I have been working out here in the garage."

Moments later, Ash came out to the garage again and said, "Gracee is gone!" I stopped what I was doing and came into the house to look around. Gracee was nowhere to be found.

"Not this again, we lost her last year and now this year?" I cried out.

Ash said, "Ask God where she is."

We all jumped into my car and while Ash was driving, I was yelling her name out the window throughout the complex. I began hearing God say to me that she found a new home and that she was safe and happy.

We continued driving on the snowy roads looking for her and yelling her name. She wasn't wearing her collar. After an hour or so driving, we came back to the apartment. Ash called the pet emergency center to see if anyone had brought in a short-legged Jack Russell within the hour. I was looking at her face when she asked the question and when she nodded her head no, I knew that she was gone.

I told Ash what had happened prior to her coming over with Gracee. Then God reminded me a year ago he had told me to watch out for this date. I sat on the couch and prayed that God had found her a home and that she would be safe and out of the snow. There was nothing more I could do but trust God.

The next morning, I called down to the office to let the staff know that Gracee was missing. The worker asked me to send him a picture of her. He told me that he would send an email out to all the residents in the complex asking if they had seen her. I gave him my phone number and asked him to call me right away if he heard anything.

I was driving to the mall to do a little Christmas shopping. On my way there, I prayed that if God wanted me to have Gracee, he would bring her back but if it was his will to have her find a new home then I would accept it.

Strolling through an aisle in one of the stores, my phone rang. When I answered I heard, "I think we have Gracee." He described her to the exact description. He told me that two ladies had found her the night before. They had given her a bath, a manicure, and placed her in a sweater.

Shocked to hear that the two ladies did all that to a dog they barely knew, I said to God, "Well, maybe they would like to keep her. Obviously they like her to go to all the trouble in taking care of her." I left the mall to head back to the office to retrieve my dog.

When I walked in, Gracee turned immediately toward the door running and wagging her tail. She was happy to see me. The ladies seemed very nice. We talked for a few moments and then we all started walking out the door.

After leaving the door of the office and standing outside, I asked the ladies if they were looking for a dog. They both looked at each other and nodded their heads yes. I had explained my situation to them and told them that Gracee was a pure-bred and that if they wanted to keep her that I would be willing to give Gracee to them at no cost along with her papers.

The ladies wanted to think about my offer, so I gave them my number and told them to let me know what they decide.

I brought Gracee back to the apartment. As I sat on the couch, she jumped up onto my lap. I gave her hugs and told her that I was glad she was safe and that I guess God had brought you back to me for a reason. I kept her sweater on as she seemed to like it.

After watching a program, I had a feeling to look for her papers just in case that if the ladies decided to take Gracee, I would be prepared. A few times before I had looked for her papers but never could find them. Searching my file box, my desk drawers, drawers in the kitchen, and in other boxes, no papers were found. I even had looked into the initial paperwork folder that we had received from the veterinarian that had her shot records.

Deciding to take one more look, I walked into the bedroom. My phone rang and looking down to see who it was. It was a number that I didn't recognize. Answering it, I heard a woman's voice. It was one of the ladies who I had spoken to early about Gracee. She asked if I would still be willing to surrender Gracee over to them. With a smile on my face and knowing that this was the right thing to do for Gracee, I agreed to. We set up a time that evening that we would exchange Gracee and all her belongings. After hanging up, I reached for that initial folder and pulled out every letter. Slowly going through each page carefully page by page, a little envelope fell out in between papers. Opening it up there were her papers! Smiling and thanking God for taking care of Gracee, I had more confidence in him knowing that if he would take care of Gracee, he would take care of me.

Later that evening, the ladies came to pick up Gracee. Seeing that Gracee was happy to see her new owners again, Ash and I knew that this was right for both parties. Ash and the boys had come over to say goodbye to Gracee. We each gave her one last hug and kiss and told her to be happy and that we would always love her.

Shutting the door, I couldn't help but tear up. Adam had given Gracee to me as a present years ago, but with our history, I knew it was time to close the chapter to my life and that included Gracee too.

KNOCK! KNOCK!

LYING IN BED, I HEARD, "IT'S TIME. It's time."

"Time for what?"

"It's time to reach out to Adam and ask him to come to Colorado."

"Okay."

Getting out of bed and getting into the shower, I let the water pour over my body. Kneeling and asking God for wisdom and strength to get me through what I was about to do, Jesus reassured me that he would be there along with me.

After finishing getting ready, I wrote him an email asking him if he could come in before the holiday to see the boys and to see me. He responded back that he thought he could make the time and gave me the date December twenty-first. It was still a couple of weeks away.

With the holidays approaching, Ash and I finished our shopping together for the boys. It really didn't feel like Christmas, but I promised myself that I would make it the best that I could.

I was working on the schedule for the following week, the week that Adam was to arrive. In scheduling myself on the twentieth, something felt off. With the feeling that I was getting I removed myself off the twentieth but added me on the twenty-first instead.

Anticipating and staying in deep prayer the following days, so I could listen for God to draw strength, I fasted for two days. During those days, I journaled and rehearsed all that I needed to say to him. God kept saying to me, "You do this, I take it from here. Trust me."

I woke up the morning of the twentieth feeling as if Adam was on his way. I know he had told me it would be the twenty-first, but knowing Adam the way I do, he always had the need to take control of everything. I knew he would come in a day earlier.

Pulling out the packet and placing the copy that needed to be signed by him, I placed the papers on the kitchen counter turned over. It had been over hundred days of not seeing him so the thought of seeing him face to face really scared me. The vision I had seen in 2015 flashed before me once again, and I knew at that moment this was the vision that God had made me feel and had been preparing me for over the years.

To keep my mind off the idea of serving divorce papers, I worked on a puzzle to keep me busy throughout the day.

Later in the afternoon, I heard a knock at my door. Looking up from placing a piece of the puzzle, I walked over to the door to look out the peephole. It was covered up so I wouldn't be able to see who it was. I knew then instantly it was Adam.

Opening the door slowly and seeing it was him, my stomach turned. He greeted me with a smile as he walked in. He reached to give me a hug but the feeling from his hug was standoffish and cold. I thought, "This will be easy." He looked around and took in all the Christmas decorating.

"It looks nice in here," he said, sitting down on the couch.

"Thank you," I said as I sat down sitting Indian style on the couch facing him.

Silence was broken by him asking me about Gracee. The emergency center sent him an email letting him know that she had went missing. So I told him the story.

I flat out asked him where we stood. He gave me the same dialogue as he did before. After hearing that I said, "I am done. I can't do this anymore."

He looked at me and said, "Okay, I guess I am going to leave." He got up and headed for the door, but I told him to hold on that I had something for him. I asked him to sit back down. I walked into the kitchen and picked up the packet and went and sat next to him.

"Could you call Loren up right now and tell her that it is over between the two of you?"

"Yes, but I wouldn't be back the right way."

"Okay," I proceeded to say. "We got married at the courthouse, so I went down to the courthouse to see how much it would cost if we were to divorce." I handed him the papers.

"What is this?" he asked. He was looking through them and then realized that all my areas were signed for a divorce.

He looked up at me while he was laying them on the couch and said, "I am not signing them."

"Yeah, I figured you would say that. Adam, it has been forty-five months since you have been with her. I can't do this anymore. All you do is think of yourself and what your needs are. When you took her to the wedding, that was my last straw. You didn't even think or care on how any of this would affect me. God has given you everything you want, a good paying job, freedom to buy anything you want, a wife who has loved you unconditionally through all your pain and has fought for your soul. You are still looking for something that only God can provide for you, and that is peace. I have done all that I can do but I want to be free so I can find someone in my life who wants to be with me as you have found yours. I guarantee that you would have never stayed with me if I was doing this to you. I know you have made your choice. Please set me free! I am making it easy on you and setting you free."

He finally got up from the couch with the papers in his hand and said in a cocky voice, "Give me a pen!"

He walked over to the kitchen table. I gave him the pen and said, "Thank you. This isn't what I want but since you are not willing to do what it takes to save our marriage, you leave me with no choice. Now you can tell Loren you are free, and you can marry her. You basically have already."

He looked up and said, "I am not telling her anything. I am setting you free. Now you can do anything you want," he said. Firing back with a no-care attitude.

THE VOICE OF FAITH

Meanwhile, God kept saying to me, "You do this, I take it from here."

Trying not to cry watching him sign the paperwork, it took all the strength in me I had. I had surrendered completely to God at that point and listened to him.

He was taking his time filling out the papers, leaving some spaces blank. "I need to get you these numbers before you can file," he said to me after reviewing what he signed.

"That's okay, I will take what I have down to the courthouse and when we have mediation, we can clear anything up. The papers will be taken down after the holidays."

He threw the pen down, stood up and pushed the chair in, and said, "I will be back next month to get the rest of my things."

"Okay, your things are out in the garage packed up for you so it will be easy. See, I am making it easy for you. I am freeing your soul. Now you don't have to feel guilty anymore or keep me guessing."

As he was walking to the door to leave, I said, "Oh, I have one more thing for you." Walking to the kitchen counter, reaching into a tray, where I had placed all our wedding rings, I placed them into his hands.

"What do you want me to do with these?" he asked.

"I don't care, pawn them, get money and buy more coins that you want so bad. I have no use for them. They mean nothing to me anymore." He put them back into the tray and turned and walked to the door.

As he turned the knob to leave, he looked at me and said, "Chow!"

He closed the door and I walked over to lock it and burst into tears. I could hear God faintly say to me, "I am so proud of you. I will take it from here." I ran into my bedroom and threw myself onto the bed and kept repeating, "It will be okay, it will be okay. I had to do this."

Crying out to God to please help me. I reached for my phone to call Felicia. I heard a knock at the door...

About the Author

HEATHER M. LARRIBAS GREW UP IN MICHIGAN
and moved to Colorado Springs over eighteen
years ago. She has three children and five grandchildren and owns a successful business for over
ten years. All of her life, she would journal and
write. She was inspired to write and share her
books based on her true story and her visions
that God shared with her. Heather wants anyone who is struggling with their, faith, themselves, relationships, marriages or abuse to be
inspired and to know that God has never left you.

CPSIA information can be obtained
at www.ICGtesting.com
Printed in the USA
LVHW042208251119
638498LV00005B/540/P